Trout Cookbook

TROUT COOKBOOK

A. D. Livingston

STACKPOLE
BOOKS

Published by
STACKPOLE BOOKS
5067 Ritter Road
Mechanicsburg, PA 17055

Printed in the United States of America

Cover design by Mark Olszewski with Caroline M. Miller

First Edition

10 9 8 7 6 5 4 3 2 1

Other Stackpole books by A. D. Livingston: *Venison Cookbook, Wild Turkey Cookbook,* and *Bass Cookbook.*

Library of Congress Cataloging-in-Publication Data

Livingston, A. D., 1932–
    Trout cookbook / A. D. Livingston. — 1st ed.
        p.   cm.
    Includes index.
    ISBN 0-8117-2581-2
    1. Cookery (Trout)   I. Title.
TX748.T74L58   1996
641.6'92—dc20   95-35527
                                                                                   CIP

Portions of this book were previously published, in a slightly different form, in the author's regular column in *Gray's Sporting Journal* and in articles that first appeared in *Sports Afield*. The author is indebted to many writers, sportsmen, cooks, and friends—all of whom are appropriately acknowledged in the text—and to his family, who provided the fish and helped test the recipes.

CONTENTS

INTRODUCTION

Sylvia Bashline, foods columnist for *Outdoor Life* magazine, once said, "A. D. Livingston enjoys cooking and it shows." It's true that I enjoy it, and I would indeed like to think that it shows in my writings on the subject. But other critics and a number of disgruntled women who write letters to publishers and editors of magazines seem to think rather strongly that I am on the argumentative side, and curmudgeonly, and sharply opinionated. Those charges are also true, I suppose. And, yes, I admit that I do enjoy this reputation. In fact, I can think of few pleasures of the fraternal sort that would beat sitting around the table at Choctawhatchee Lodge (where I used to cook a dish or two for hunters) and arguing, after the repast, the merits of cooking fish by this method or that, concluding just short of a fist fight with a Texan or a New Hampshirite.

My wife still doesn't understand it, but I like to believe that I have a reason for being the way I am. If I say, for example, that yellow cornmeal is unfit for human consumption, the reader who is unfamiliar with my work should know that I may be stretching it a bit in order to elicit a response from another cook or food lover or critic. Thus, I can find out not only what the sport believes but also how strongly he believes it.

—A.D. Livingston

ONE

Trout in the Skillet

Let's get right into the heat of things with two quotes, one from author Angus Cameron's version of the late L. L. Bean's philosophy of trout cookery and another from Auguste Escoffier, the famous French chef and cookbook writer:

> The operation consists of cooking the fish (or slices or fillets of fish) in the frying-pan with very hot butter. . . .
> —*The Escoffier Cook Book*

> Mr. Bean's personal recipe for brook trout shows that he knew the secret of slow cookery for fish.
> —*The L. L. Bean Game & Fish Cookbook*

What we have here isn't merely a failure to communicate; it's a clear-cut disagreement, simply because you can't cook a fish slowly in very hot butter. I could, I suppose, explain the discrepancy away on practical grounds, saying that Escoffier was no doubt using clarified butter and a heavy skillet, both of which will take a high heat, whereas Bean was probably cooking over a bed of coals somewhere in the backwoods of Maine on a little folding lightweight camp skillet, which tends to burn things. But this would be mere conjecture on my part. I suppose that I should also try to distinguish between deep frying and pan frying, pointing out that fish cooked in a small amount of oil or butter at low heat is sautéed, not fried. But I'm not inclined to go this way, either, because most of us like to think that we fry trout and sauté mushrooms. Instead of trying to reconcile the two positions, I'll

1

simply say that both men are wrong on several counts, which I'll get to in due course.

The plain truth is that both methods are good, provided that they are done properly. I feel, however, that the low-heat method tends to soak up more butter or oil, which isn't good for your health, according to current thinking. On the other hand, proponents of the low-heat method usually start with only a small amount of butter or oil in the skillet, so there's not much to soak up. Some experts want all of the butter and will even pour what's left in the skillet over the fish or use it to make a butter sauce.

I'll eat in either camp, and I can sometimes tell beforehand what I'm going to get. If the cook breaks out a Teflon-coated skillet, for example, I know that he is of the low-heat, long-cooking school; if he goes with cast iron, I can expect the skillet to sizzle. But if I'm cooking, I prefer to use quite a bit of hot oil in the skillet, thereby splitting the difference between skillet frying and deep frying. My recipe is set forth toward the end of this chapter, if you care to read that far, but perhaps my best advice is for you to master all the techniques. After all, L. L. Bean's method may come in handy when you're wading a stream and don't want to lug along a quart of peanut oil and a heavy-duty cast-iron skillet. My method may suit you better if you are cooking on the tailgate of your pickup truck.

The recipes below all call for a specific oil and coating. A more general discussion of cooking oils and coatings for fish appears in the next chapter, about deep frying.

L. L. Bean's Brook Trout

In addition to saying that the late L. L. Bean knew the secret of skillet cooking a fish slowly, Angus Cameron and Judith Jones, coauthors of the book, quoted the mail-order magnate as saying that pork fat is much better than bacon fat or butter for frying trout. Apparently Bean meant fat rendered from fresh pork. Reportedly, Bean also said that flour is much better than cornmeal for frying fish.

Well . . . a lot of people, including this writer, could take issue with these statements, saying that peanut oil is the best for frying, and fine cornmeal is definitely better than flour. All such statements, on both sides, should be qualified. If, for example, you want to cook on high heat, peanut oil is very hard to beat, because it has a high smoking point. Also, cornmeal doesn't burn as easily as flour, so it is better in this regard. But to be really good as a coating, the cornmeal should be of the right kind—that is, fine stone-ground meal made from whole-kernel corn. Most of the commercial cornmeals sold in this country, however, are coarse and downright gritty. The coarse meals available in Maine (I would guess) wouldn't stick very well to the fish without the aid of chicken eggs or other goo, so L. L., a sensible fellow, used flour for dusting the trout. The angler in the Deep South, on the other hand, tended to use a fine-ground whole-kernel corn-meal, widely available a few decades ago at the small gristmills within a buggy ride from many southern towns. The millponds, I might add, were popular fishing holes before the large im-poundments were built in this country, and were the site of many family and community fish fries.

Before getting to Bean's recipe, I might also add that he reportedly said to cut the heads off the trout, a statement that surely cost him some business in New York State and is still sure to bring harsh words from some quarters. In any case, here's his recipe and method.

> brook trout
> pork fat
> flour
> salt

After dressing the trout, fry out a liberal amount of pork fat. Add a little salt to the flour, then roll the trout in the mix. Fry the trout slowly until they are crisp and nicely browned. Place the trout on a hot platter lined with clean paper to absorb the fat. Serve with sliced lemon for those who want it.

Note: L. L. Bean didn't say so, but the residue left when the pork is fried can be used in southern-style corn bread, called crackling bread. If you don't have a good crackling bread recipe, sprinkle the cracklings on tossed salads or over sour-cream-topped baked potatoes. The stuff is too good to throw away.

If you don't have fatty pork to render and don't want to buy a Boston butt, you can still buy rendered hog fat at the market. It's called lard, and only a few years ago it was the major cooking oil used in this country. It is still hard to beat for baking some recipes (especially delicate pastries), but most modern health authorities frown heavily on its use.

L. L. Bean notwithstanding, bacon and trout make good sense for the streamside cook. If you don't catch a trout, eat the bacon. If you catch fish, eat both. Salt pork can also be used instead of bacon.

Trout According to George Herter

George Leonard Herter, also a bull cook of mail-order fame, used a combination of butter and beef suet to pan-fry fish. The beef suet, he said, kept the butter from turning too dark. Herter was also fond of pan-frying steaks in beef suet, a fat that can be used on high heat without burning. For more of Herter, see Mormon Trout on page 67.

Trout According to Bradford Angier

Here's another man with firm opinions about how to cook a trout. For brook trout, he says, open the fish as soon as possible and remove the liver and roe if you can use them immediately. Leave the heads on unless somebody objects violently. Heat ½ stick of butter in a skillet, and sauté the trout, browning it on both sides. Cook the roe and liver at the same time. Use no batter. Use no flour. Use no cornmeal. Angier says he likes the crispy skin as is and feels that cornmeal has an unpleasant toughening effect.

Transfer the cooked fish to a hot serving platter and sprinkle on a little salt. If you want a sauce, he says, let the pan cool just a little from the frying temperature, then add 2 teaspoons vinegar, 4 teaspoons chopped fresh parsley, and maybe 2 teaspoons of chopped capers. Cook and stir until the sauce is brown, then pour it over the hot trout. Serve with lemon wedges, and place a few freshly washed parsley sprigs beside the trout if you want a garnish.

The same recipe can be used for lake trout fillets, as well as for whole small brook trout.

Note: I have no quarrel with frying fish without flour or cornmeal, but be warned that undusted trout fried at a high temperature tend to stick. The exception is the blackened redfish, cooked on extremely hot cast-iron griddles without any grease or without any coating except for a crust of hot pepper, paprika, and other seasonings.

Italian Trout

This surprisingly simple recipe is also for pan-frying fish without any coating whatsoever. I find it to be a very good streamside recipe simply because it requires few ingredients—and because it is so good that you'll fish even harder after lunch. It's best to have a good spatula on hand. Also, because the salt is applied after cooking, I recommend this recipe for anyone on a low-salt diet.

> small trout or fillets
> olive oil
> lemons (for juice)
> salt

Pan-dress the fish. Heat a little olive oil in a heavy skillet, and cook the fish on both sides for a few minutes, until the fish flakes easily. Sprinkle each serving lightly with salt and fresh lemon juice. Lemon slices and quarters look nice, but I like mine cut in half so that they're easier to squeeze.

Variation: Mix garlic-flavored olive oil half-and-half with the regular olive oil.

5

Sautéed Trout

Here's yet another good recipe for pan-cooking a trout or two without the aid of flour or meal.

> 1 or 2 trout, 1 pound each or less, dressed whole
> ½ cup milk
> salt
> 2 strips bacon
> 1 tablespoon white wine Worcestershire sauce
> 2 or 3 green onions, chopped with part of tops

Dissolve 1 teaspoon salt in the milk, and dip the trout in the liquid, coating all over. Fry the bacon in the skillet, and remove it to drain. Heat the skillet until the bacon drippings are almost to the smoking point. Place the trout in the skillet, and cook on both sides until the meat flakes easily when tested with a fork. It's best to turn the fish only once. If the fat gets too hot, remove the skillet from the heat for a minute or two and turn down the heat a little.

Put the fish onto a brown bag to drain. Sauté the chopped onion in the remaining bacon grease for about 5 minutes. Then stir in the white wine Worcestershire sauce. Add a little salt to taste. Crumble the pieces of bacon and stir them in. Place the fish on plates, then pour the sauce over them.

Trout Meunière

Fish meunière, a French formula, is popular in New Orleans, where it is used with a Gulf Coast spotted sea trout (similar to the weakfish), and in Quebec, where it is used with brook trout. The French prepare a special sauce meunière and apply it to broiled fish or possibly other forms of cooked fish. Americans tend to pan-fry the trout in butter, then stir up a sauce in the pan drippings.

4 brook trout
¾ cup butter
½ cup chopped parsley
juice of 1 lemon
heavy cream
flour
salt and pepper

Melt the butter in a skillet and bring to heat—but not to the smoking point. Meanwhile, warm a serving platter. Sprinkle the dressed fish inside and out with salt and pepper. Roll the fish in heavy cream, then sprinkle with flour. Sauté the fish on both sides until the meat flakes easily when tested with a fork. Remove the fish from the skillet, and place them on a heated serving platter. The butter left in the pan should be a little brown. If it isn't, cook it a little longer. Stir in the pan drippings and add the lemon juice and chopped parsley. Cook and stir for a minute or two, shaking the pan, then pour the sauce over the fish. Eat hot.

Summer Savory Trout

If you are tired of parsley, try adding some fresh summer savory to your sautéed trout. A member of the mint family, the herb adds a fresh, slightly piquant flavor.

small whole trout or fillets
butter
flour
milk
fresh summer savory, chopped
salt and pepper

Heat the butter in a skillet. Dip the trout or fillets in milk, sprinkle them with salt and pepper, roll them in flour, and sauté them until browned on both sides, turning only once. After turning, sprinkle on a little of the summer savory.

Trout with Fiddleheads

Never miss the opportunity to gather a mess of fiddleheads from
the ostrich fern *(Matteuccia struthiopteris)* whenever you run across
them in the forests or along a stream in the Northeast. You may
even find them for sale in a market, fresh, canned, or frozen. They
are best, I think, when first steamed or poached and then sautéed
quickly in butter—which fits right in with pan-fried trout.

> trout
> fiddleheads
> butter
> all-purpose flour
> salt and pepper

If you have fresh ferns, cut off the bases and carefully remove
the furry brown covering. Wash the fiddleheads, drop them into
a pot of boiling salted water, and cook for 5 minutes. Drain. Melt
some butter in a skillet. Salt and pepper the trout to taste, dredge
in flour, and sauté in butter until browned on both sides. Carefully remove the trout and drain on a heated platter. Add more
butter to the skillet if needed, then quickly sauté the fiddleheads.
Serve hot. The fiddleheads can be boiled ahead of time. (If you
are using canned fiddleheads, remember that these are precooked
and should be merely drained, washed, and sautéed briefly.)

Note: Some authorities warn that some ferns produce fiddleheads that are carcinogenic. These suspects include the ubiqui-
tous bracken fern, which is commonly eaten in Europe, Asia, New
Zealand, Japan, and North America. In spite of the warnings of
carcinogenic properties, I'll eat fiddleheads from any fern, including the bracken, but I do so in moderation. The small fiddleheads
are safer and also make the best eating.

The American Indians ate fiddleheads raw before a hunt so
that they would smell like the fern, a favorite deer food. The Indians
also made bread from the roots of the bracken fern. In the Northwest, they peeled the roots of the sword fern and baked them with
salmon eggs in pits in the ground, much like the New England
clambake.

Wild Onion Trout

Wild onions are plentiful in most sections of this country. There are a number of varieties, many of which have a narrow stem like chives. In this recipe, I use the small bulbs and about half of the green tops. Be warned that some of the wild onions and garlics are quite strong and should be used sparingly.

>4 skillet-sized trout
>flour
>1 cup butter (divided)
>⅓ to ½ cup minced wild green onions with part of tops
>juice of 1 large lemon or lime
>salt and pepper

Dress the trout for pan frying. Sprinkle with salt and pepper, then roll or shake in flour. Heat half the butter in a skillet, and cook the trout until browned on both sides. Remove the trout to a brown bag to drain, then place them on a heated serving platter. Add the other half of the butter to the skillet. Sauté the wild onions for 5 minutes. Stir in the lemon or lime juice, then pour the sauce over the trout. Serve hot.

Note: This is a good recipe for cooking in camp while wild onions are in season.

Davis Dust

Although I sometimes think we ought to reduce our recipes to the basic ingredients, there are some people in this country who feel a genuine need to add stuff at every opportunity. Cajuns are especially good at this. A New Orleans culinary sport by the name of Frank Davis, author of *The Frank Davis Seafood Notebook*, came up with a spiced dusting mix that he says will really perk up the flavor of the ordinary salt, pepper, and cornmeal (or flour) mix. The measurements call for dashes and pinches, and I have not tried to be more exact. A pinch is pretty much the amount of dry stuff that can be removed between the thumb and forefinger, but a dash leaves me puzzled. In any case, it is less than can be easily determined with standard measuring spoons, and I generally take it to be a good deal less than ⅛ teaspoon. A pat of butter is a little square piece served in New Orleans restaurants. Anyhow, I have broken the recipe into two parts.

Davis Dust
1 cup cornmeal or flour
1 tablespoon salt
1 teaspoon onion powder
½ teaspoon white pepper
½ teaspoon celery salt
¼ teaspoon cayenne
¼ teaspoon McCormick lemon pepper
a dash of mace
a pinch of powdered mustard

Mix all of the ingredients thoroughly, then put in a bowl or shaker for dusting or a small brown bag for shaking. I prefer the latter method.

The Fish
small whole trout or fillets
Davis Dust (above)
1 cup milk in a bowl
oil
1 pat unsalted butter

Dress the fish and rig for pan frying, heating a little oil with a pat of butter. Either dust the fillets with the coating mixture or shake them in a bag. Dip each piece into the milk, then shake it again in the bag. Pan-fry immediately, browning nicely on both sides.

Hahatonka Lodge Rainbows

I found this recipe in *Cy Littlebee's Guide to Cooking Fish & Game*, published by the Missouri Department of Conservation. Cy says he got the recipe from Mrs. Leroy J. Snyder, who says it's the way they fry rainbows at Hahatonka Lodge on Lake of the Ozarks. Cy says it's mighty fine, then quotes Mrs. Snyder, who seems to be fond of making her points with capital letters:

"See that the trout are VERY clean inside. Do NOT scale trout. DO NOT CUT OFF THE HEAD OR THE TAIL. Salt and pepper inside and outside, then roll in flour. Do not use cornmeal. Use fresh Crisco, and never use that Crisco again to fry trout. Allow shortening to become very hot in skillet. Use about as much shortening as will come up to about ⅔ of the fish's thickness; in other words, do not fry fish in deep fat. For trout that weigh about ½ or ¾ of a pound, fry fish no longer than 5 minutes on each side. If trout are cooked too long you cannot remove the backbone plus head and tail in one piece, together with the side bones. If trout are fried correctly, by pushing the delicate meat gently off each side of the fish, you can pick up the tail of the fish and all the bones, including the head, will come out in one piece. In this way you won't get a mouthful of bones. Rainbow trout cooked correctly only have ONE bone. If you remove the head and tail before cooking, you cannot accomplish this."

Livingston's Skillet Fry

Here's my favorite way of frying trout, as well as most other fish. I use a 12-inch (or larger) cast-iron skillet, and I fill it with peanut oil to a depth that almost, but not quite, covers the fish I'm going to fry. This method rather splits the difference between pan frying and deep frying (discussed in the next chapter) and, I like to think, retains some of the advantages of both. I get the oil very hot, almost to the smoking point, and I use a fine stone-ground whole-kernel cornmeal. Although I prefer white meal, the color isn't as important as the way the corn is processed and ground. See chapter 13 for a longer discussion of cornmeal, which is also used in the hush puppies that so many Americans expect with fried fish.

> trout
> cornmeal
> peanut oil
> salt

Dress the fish for pan frying. Heat the peanut oil in the skillet until it almost reaches the smoking point. When very hot, the oil will start to move about in the pan as heat currents develop. To test the heat, hold a mealed trout by the head and dip its tail into the oil. If it sizzles nicely, you're ready to cook. Salt and pepper the fish, then shake them, a few at a time, in a bag with the cornmeal. Remove the fish and let them sit for a minute or two so that the meal will stick. Using tongs, place the fish into the skillet. Do not crowd. Cook until browned on both sides, turning once. Drain on a brown bag. Serve hot.

In this method of cooking, the bottom part of the fish will be in direct contact with the skillet while the midsection is submerged in oil and the top part is sticking out (until it gets its turn on the bottom). The deep oil cooks the midsection of the fish, and the bottom of the skillet, which is a little hotter than the oil, will cook the bottom. The bottom gets browner, giving the fish a two-toned effect. Filling a pan too full of oil is dangerous, so do not use this method in a deep griddle or in a skillet without deep sides, and use it only for small fish or fillets, not for fish that are 2 inches thick. Larger fish should be deep-fried, as discussed in the next chapter.

TWO

Deep-Fried Trout

Although skillet frying is my favorite way of cooking trout, the method is usually impractical for feeding a crowd. On the other hand, heating a large batch of oil for deep frying is impractical when cooking for only one or two people. I do, however, heat a large batch of oil whenever I want to deep-fry whole trout that are too large for the skillet, as when making the sweet-and-sour recipe later in this chapter.

If properly done, deep frying can produce trout that are surprisingly fat-free. How can this be? Deep frying at a high temperature seals in the fish juices and seals out the oil. In this regard, deep frying may be much more healthy than sogging a trout in butter on low heat. Deep frying can be a very easy way to cook, provided that you have the right equipment and the right ingredients—and know how to use both. Here are some pointers.

1. Choose a good oil, and get enough of it. I use peanut oil because it is odorless and tasteless, it has a high smoke point, and it doesn't absorb too much taste or odor from foods cooked in it. One batch of oil will therefore do for deep-frying fish, potatoes, and hush puppies. Peanut oil is not cheap, but I buy it in 2-gallon jugs, thereby lowering the price per ounce. I have tried various other cooking oils, including canola oil, but peanut oil seems to work better for me; also, it is more economical in the long run because I can use it over and over. Olive oil can also be used successfully and is not too expensive if you buy it by the gallon instead of in little salad oil bottles.

Take care of your oil if you intend to use it again and again.

13

Avoid temperatures that heat the oil beyond the smoking point, which seems to break down the oil, discoloring it and giving it an odor. After you have finished frying your trout, let the oil cool and settle. Dip the oil out and run it through a coffee filter; I use the plastic basket from an old coffeemaker for this purpose. This process takes a little more time, but the oil comes out bright and fresh. The bottom of the deep fryer may have lots of brown sediment in it. The amount depends on what kind of batter or coating you used, and on how well the coating stuck to the fish. The coarse, gritty cornmeal usually sold in supermarkets is particularly bad about leaving sediment. You can throw this out directly from the deep fryer, or you can run it through the coffee filter to get every drop of oil.

If you are cooking only a batch or two of fish, there shouldn't be much sediment, but if you are frying several batches of fish, the accumulation can become a real problem. It helps to set the pieces of fish aside for a few minutes after dusting with a coating so that it will stick better. It also helps to dip the fish pieces in milk before dusting them with flour or meal, although I seldom do this.

Once there is too much sediment, it's difficult to continue frying. It may be best to drain the cooker, clean it, and start over, but pouring a gallon or more of very hot oil out of the fish fryer so that it can be cleaned is inconvenient, time-consuming, and dangerous. Consider instead making a long-handled wire strainer and removing the sediment from time to time as you cook. Design the strainer to work in your cooker; for example, use a square strainer for a rectangular cooker. Metal screen mesh will work for the strainer basket if you can find it, but keep in mind that a lot of screening these days is made from plastic.

Frying potatoes in used oil will freshen the oil somewhat, and I am also fond of adding several slices of fresh ginger root while I am frying the fish. I once had a neighbor who fried good fish, but he had a habit of frying the fish first, then the hush puppies, and then the potatoes. He said that the potatoes took the fish odor out of the oil. I told him that he did it exactly backward. First you fry the potatoes to get out any odor left from the last batch of fish or chicken. Next, fry the bread. Then fry the fish last

14

so that it will be hot. He told me that I may be right, but in his family they fried the fish first. Suit yourself.

2. Use good equipment. I prefer to deep-fry fish in a container made of cast iron or heavy aluminum. Cast-iron Dutch ovens, without the top, make very good deep fryers, if you have a way to heat them; some camp stoves won't do the job. My second choice is thick aluminum or stainless steel. Thin metal cookers tend to warp. I have used several fryers coated with Teflon or some such stuff, but it always seems to come off, and the ceramic-coated metal cookers, some of which are quite expensive, are apt to crack at high temperatures.

There are some good indoor cookers designed to be used atop a kitchen stove, as well as some self-contained electrically heated deep fryers. Some of these are too small to be of much value to me, and some take too long to heat. Some (but not all) of the patio or camp cookers do a better job, and I especially like those heated with large portable rechargeable cylinders or bottles of gas. (Get two bottles.) These can be used in some camps, on the patio, or for that matter, in the kitchen. They can also be used on the tailgate of a pickup truck or some such vehicle (except that some upholstered tailgates these days are a little too fancy for cooking purposes) or on a pontoon boat. Consider buying a patio cooker that is rectangular instead of round for poaching large fish. On the other hand, a round cooker is better suited for large stock pots. Get one of each. In either case, it's best to use a pot that is at least 6 inches deep.

For cooking larger batches, you can use cast-iron wash pots or even the large vats used for scalding hogs. Remember that uneven heating can cause large cast-iron vessels to crack. Never put a cold pot over a very hot fire. Heat and cool it slowly. I have seen several cookers, designed for feeding a hundred or more people, built on boat trailers for portability. Sometimes these can be borrowed or rented.

On a smaller scale, a number of cast-iron and aluminum cookers are designed for use on a stove. Most of these are circular, but some are oval or rectangular, made for heating over two stove burners. Almost all of these have lids, but I don't recommend that lids be used for frying fish, potatoes, or hush puppies.

Deep frying with hot oil is a hands-on kind of cooking, in which you need to see what you are doing—and hear the fish cooking—and smell the good fried-fish aroma. Anyone who doesn't want to smell fish cooking in the house can go out into the yard.

3. *Use coatings sparingly.* A light dusting of cornmeal, flour, or some such coating gives fried fish a good color and crunch; it also helps keep the fish juices in and the oil out. A thicker coating or batter might accomplish these things and produce even more crunch, but it is also a grease trap. I can't see it any other way. If, however, you prefer a thick batter or don't have enough fish to feed everybody, then use it. A few of the recipes below do call for batter, although I don't advise it. A batter is a mixture of milk or egg, flour, and other substances. The fish is dipped into it, then dropped into hot oil. Although it produces a thick crust, a batter also tends to stick to your hands or drip everywhere or both. At least, this has been my experience. (While writing this chapter, I decided to take a new look at batters and cooked up a recipe using Aunt Jemima pancake mix and 7-Up. It was a wretched mess.) As a rule, a batter works better with the deep-frying technique than with a skillet; the bottom of the skillet causes the batter to flatten out and tends to burn it.

A good many recipes also call for coating a fish in beaten egg, milk, or some other substance, then rolling it in flour, cornmeal, cracker crumbs, or other coating or combination of coatings. The egg is used to pick up more of the dry coating and help it stick to the fish. Some people first roll the fish in a coating, dip it into egg, then roll it again in the coating. This picks up even more coating and approaches a batter in thickness and messiness.

My favorite method of coating fish is to put some fine stone-ground whole-kernel cornmeal into a bag, then shake the fish in it. I remove the fish from the bag and shake off the excess cornmeal; then I set the fish aside for a few minutes before frying. This helps the meal stick to the fish, which can be very important if you are frying several batches to feed a crowd. Note that I do not add salt and pepper to the cornmeal. I usually sprinkle each fish or fillet on both sides with a little salt and pepper before I shake it in cornmeal. (If I am using cayenne, however, I put it into the meal, because it's difficult to sprinkle a small amount evenly.) After I finish coating all the fish, I don't throw out the bag of meal. I close it securely and put it in the freezer. The next time I fry fish, I use this bag plus a little new meal. I normally apply a flour coating in the same way, rather than rolling the fish in it or sprinkling it on. This method is less messy and does an excellent job.

When you choose a coating for your fish, consider three properties: Does it tend to burn at high frying temperatures? Does it stick to the fish without the aid of chicken eggs or milk? (Some gritty cornmeals simply won't stick very well.) Does it brown nicely and taste good?

I'm not trying to push plain flour or cornmeal off on anyone, but what I am offering is a system for deep-frying fish that works. It's quick. It doesn't mess up bowls and countertops. It's consistent. And it's very easy if you get the procedure and the equipment and the ingredients down pat. If you'd rather sop your fish in sticky flour goo, get batter all over your hands, mess up bowls and containers to be washed, and fry fish that absorb lots of grease, have at it.

4. Get the right temperature and hold it. The success of deep frying depends on getting a sufficient amount of oil very hot and then plunging the fish into it. How hot? At least 375 degrees. Small fish and thin fillets or fingers can be cooked at a hotter temperature—even as high as 450 degrees, if you've got an oil that can take the heat. Small fish or thin fillets will cook very quickly. Larger fish or thicker fillets require longer cooking at a lower temperature so that the inside will get done before the outside burns.

To reach a high temperature quickly, you need an adequate heating system, and some camp stoves simply won't do the job. My stove-top deep fryer will work, but it takes a long time to heat the oil. A heavy-duty self-standing fryer, heated with a large, portable tank of gas, is ideal.

The expert can tell when his oil is hot enough to cook. The oil will start moving about, as if getting ready to boil; a current actually develops as the hot oil rises to the top. There are various ways of testing the oil, such as holding a floured or mealed fish by the head and dipping its tail into the oil. If it bubbles nicely, the oil is ready for cooking.

After you get the oil hot, it is important to keep it hot. To this end, you need to either use a large amount of oil or cook a small amount of fish at a time. Putting in too many fish at one time will cool the oil too much.

5. *Choose a good oil thermometer.* Regardless of your experience, you will benefit by having a good oil thermometer to use in your deep fryer. It helps to know how much the temperature changes when you add a batch of fish. With this information, you will know approximately how many fish, french fries, and hush puppies to add at a time, and when to increase or decrease the heat with the gas flow valve or thermostat.

There are several thermometers on the market that can be used in a deep fryer. My favorite is a dial thermometer that clamps to the side of the fryer. The clamp is adjustable, so that you can vary the depth of the probe. The thermometer should read up to at least 400 degrees, preferably to 550 degrees. I think it's best to avoid the old glass mercury column thermometers at high temperatures.

6. *Use the proper utensils.* Many deep fryers come with baskets for holding the food to be fried. I use these for french fries but never for fish, except possibly for whitebait (tiny fish fried whole, guts and all). The trouble with metal baskets is that they lower the temperature of the oil drastically when they are submerged. Of course, you can submerge them in the oil and allow them to heat up before putting in the fish, then use them to remove the fish. Nevertheless, it takes longer to drain the cooked fish—and they may not drain properly.

To put the fish into a deep fryer of normal size, it's best to add one piece at a time with tongs. I admit that I sometimes add the fish by hand, holding them by the tail and easing them in headfirst, but tongs are safer. Never use a fork. You will tear your fish and drop it into the hot grease, which can badly burn your hand or worse.

When a fish is done, it will float to the surface. I usually let mine cook a few seconds longer, then remove it with a spatula.

This is done on an individual basis, simply because no two pieces of fish are exactly alike. A flat strainer, or skimmer, also can be used, and many people prefer these.

7. *Don't overcook your fish—but get them done.* If your grease is at the right temperature, your fish will be done when they look brown and crunchy on the outside. If the temperature is too low, your fish might well dry out before the outside browns. Remember that a large percentage of the fish is water. Water boils at 212 degrees (at sea level), and as you're frying at 375 degrees or better, you can dry out the flesh.

Overcooking fish is more common than undercooking. This is especially true of people who don't fish or hunt, since they tend to view anything wild with suspicion. Undercooking in a deep fryer usually happens with large whole fish. These should be cooked at a lower temperature for a longer period of time. I have, however, cooked them at very high temperatures (to get a crusty surface) by first scoring the trout on both sides. Cut diagonal gashes down to the backbone, spacing the cuts about 3 inches apart.

8. *Drain fried trout properly.* All fried fish will drip when you remove it from the grease. The better you drain the fish, the more palatable it will be (unless you have cooked it in butter and love the taste of it). I like to remove a piece of fish with tongs and drain it over the cooker for a few seconds, shaking it a little, before putting it aside to drain. Absorbent paper should be used, and I prefer ordinary brown grocery bags. If I am cooking a large batch of fish, I will drain a few on one end, then pile them on the other end. Never pile undrained fried fish on a platter; the bottom layer will become soggy.

9. *Keep the fish hot, and eat them quickly.* Cook first the potatoes, then the bread, then the fish. All of these can be kept warm, up to a point, on brown bags. Use two thicknesses on the bottom, then top with another bag to hold in the heat. A heated platter or serving tray can also be used under the brown bag or absorbent paper, but leave the fish on the paper until serving time. I normally put the brown bag on a wooden chopping block and put the whole works onto the table. Then it's every man for

himself. Occasionally we transfer the fish to a platter for a more formal table setting.

Merely keeping the fried fish hot is not enough; they quickly lose their crunch. The fish should be eaten as soon as they are taken out of the deep fryer, being allowed to cool down a little on individual plates.

10. Be safe. Hot oil is dangerous. The more you have, the greater the danger. Oil that gets too hot can burst into flames; this is especially true with stove-top skillets that are too full of oil. If left unattended, the oil can boil over onto the hot stove burner or fire, flaming up and causing the oil in the skillet to blaze up. Do not try to douse the flames with water. Do not try to remove a burning skillet or other fryer from the house; when you open the outside door, a sudden rush of air can blow the flames back on your hands, burning you and causing you to drop the burning grease onto the floor.

Instead, put out the fire with a handful of baking soda, with a fire extinguisher suitable for grease fires, or by dropping on a tight-fitting lid. I always keep several boxes of baking soda in my kitchen. When a handful of baking soda hits the hot grease, it generates carbon dioxide gas, extinguishing the fire almost instantly.

Large outdoor cookers present different hazards. Obviously, these should not be used in areas where children are playing. At large gatherings, I've seen fish fried in a large cast-iron vat designed for scalding hogs. These should be fenced off from the crowd.

In any case, here are a few recipes for you to consider. I recommend that you try them all and come up with your own favorite. My favorite deep-fry recipe was set forth in the last chapter, consisting of only four ingredients: fish, peanut oil, cornmeal, and salt. For deep frying, use a suitable rig and cook the fish in very hot grease—375 degrees or preferably hotter. This method is simple, fast, inexpensive (if you reuse the oil), and easy—and it produces good fish. But here are some other methods and ingredients that may suit you better:

Trout and Chips

This old British dish has been made with various kinds of fish, from eels to shark. Fillets from small trout can be used successfully, but the larger lake trout are not recommended for deep frying. Most modern recipes hold out for potatoes cut into fingers about ½ inch thick. These are french fries. I like to think that the original fish and chips were made from sliced potatoes; American potato chips came from this tradition, only they got thinner and thinner. In any case, my version of this recipe calls for potatoes cut into slices ¼ inch thick. (I don't peel the potatoes, but suit yourself.)

The measures below feed from 2 to 6 people. When I eat fish free for the catching, I want lots of it, so I allow ½ pound of boneless fish, or 1 pound of undressed fish, for each adult—and more for strapping boys who have participated in the catch. Most modern cookbooks don't allow this much.

The British fish and chips are usually served without bread, and the fish are sprinkled lightly with cider vinegar or malt vinegar. In England, fish and chips are sold at vending stands in several thicknesses of newspaper that have been rolled into a cone. Such a package is easy to hold and is disposable. For this reason, the recipe is a good one for serving at outdoor gatherings—especially where there are not enough tables to seat everybody. Some sources say to line the cone with waxed paper, but I can't recommend this. One important function of the newspaper is to soak up some of the grease, and waxed paper would prevent this. In this regard, even better cones can be made from brown grocery bags. These should be cut open, flattened, and rolled, using three or four thicknesses of paper.

> 1 to 2 pounds small trout fillets, boneless
> 4 to 6 medium potatoes, cut into slices ½ inch thick
> peanut oil
> 1 cup all-purpose flour
> 1 cup milk
> 1½ teaspoons baking powder
> salt and pepper
> paprika (optional)

Rig for deep frying at 375 degrees. First fry the potatoes, a few at a time, until they are lightly browned. This takes 4 or 5 minutes per batch. Spread the potatoes out on a brown bag to drain. Add another batch to the deep fryer. Sprinkle the first batch with salt, pepper, and paprika if desired, then cover the potatoes with another brown bag to help hold in the heat. When the second batch is done, move the first batch into a pile to make room for the second. While the last batch of potatoes cooks, salt and pepper the trout fillets. Mix the flour, baking powder, and milk, then beat it until you have a smooth batter. Dip the fillets into the batter, and deep-fry them a few at a time until nicely browned, which should take only 3 or 4 minutes if your oil is hot enough. Do not overcrowd the fillets. Drain the cooked fillets on a brown bag. Put a suitable amount of fish and chips in a paper cone, and provide vinegar for those who want it. Americans may prefer catsup.

Deep-Fried Trout with Batter

Although pan-frying small whole trout is something of a stream-side tradition, they can also be deep-fried successfully. This recipe calls for coating the fish with a batter.

> small trout, dressed
> 1 cup all-purpose flour
> ½ cup milk
> 2 chicken eggs
> 2 teaspoons salt
> 1 teaspoon baking powder
> cooking oil

Rig for deep frying and turn on the heat. Whisk the chicken eggs lightly, stirring in the milk as you go. In a separate bowl, mix the flour, baking powder, and salt. Stir the egg mixture into the flour mixture, then beat in 1 teaspoon of cooking oil. When the oil in the deep fryer reaches 375 degrees, dip each fish into the batter and deep-fry for a few minutes, until golden brown. If you have a large batch of fish, fry them just a few at a time (depending on the size of your fryer) so that the oil will stay very hot. Do not overcook.

I prefer to leave the head on the fish for deep frying because I like to gnaw on it, but some people want it off. Suit yourself— or, better, suit your guests. If in doubt, remove the heads, fry them separately, and gnaw on them in the privacy of your kitchen. Or save them for fish soup.

Good Ol' Boy Trout

I don't have exact measures for this recipe, but anyone who has fried many fish won't have a problem with it. I do, however, advise you to go gently on the cayenne and Tabasco, unless you have plenty of beer on ice.

> boneless trout fillets
> peanut oil
> prepared mustard
> beer
> cornmeal
> salt
> Tabasco sauce
> cayenne

Mix some beer, mustard, and Tabasco sauce in a large bowl. Add the trout fillets, tossing to coat all sides, and marinate for 1 hour. Heat about ½ inch of peanut oil in a skillet or rig for deep frying at 375 degrees. Put some cornmeal into a bag and add some salt and cayenne. Remove the fish from the marinade, then shake in the bag with the cornmeal. Shake off the excess meal, and fry quickly in hot oil. Serve hot.

Deep-Fried Trout Amandine

Generally believed to be a skillet dish, trout amandine is also good if the trout is deep-fried, then topped with an amandine sauce. Rig for deep frying at 375 degrees or higher. While the oil is heating, get the ingredients ready for the sauce. It's best to cook fish and sauce at the same time, if you can work it out, so that neither gets cold while waiting for the other. I usually ask my wife to start cooking the sauce while I start the fish. Remember that heating the oil for deep frying takes more time than the cooking. You'll need lots of oil in a rather large container to cook whole trout properly. This recipe is for 3 or 4 trout. The fish should be about 12 or 13 inches long, dressed with head and tail left on.

Amandine Sauce
1 cup slivered almonds
1 cup salted butter
juice of 1 lemon
½ teaspoon freshly ground black pepper

Melt the butter in a cast-iron skillet, and heat it until it turns slightly brown. Add the almonds and cook for 1½ minutes, shaking the skillet as they cook. Remove the skillet from the heat. Add the lemon juice and pepper, stirring with a wooden spoon. Put the skillet back on the heat for 1 minute. Serve the sauce hot over the trout.

The Trout
3 or 4 trout, heads on, about 12 or 13 inches long
½ cup flour
milk
1 teaspoon salt
⅛ teaspoon black pepper
⅛ teaspoon cayenne
peanut oil

Make sure the oil reaches 375 degrees or a little hotter. Score the trout 3 times diagonally on each side. Mix the flour, salt, black pepper, and cayenne in a long shallow pan. Put the milk in a container. Dip each trout in the milk, then quickly roll it in the seasoned flour. Put the fish into the hot oil, and fry until nicely browned. As a rule, the fish is done when it floats, but I usually give it a few more seconds to brown nicely. Serve the fish on individual plates or platters, topped with the Amandine Sauce. Add lemon wedges as a garnish.

Note: Deep-fried trout amandine is a good dish for feeding a crowd of 15 or 20 people, if you have one or more large deep fryers available. The fish can be cooked on the patio, and a large batch (or batches) of sauce can be prepared in the kitchen, using a large jambalaya skillet or an electric skillet or two.

Sweet-and-Sour Trout

For cooking this dish, you'll need a deep fryer long enough to accommodate whole trout 11 or 12 inches long. The fryer should also be deep enough to hold sufficient oil to float the cooked fish and to fry at high heat safely. A large patio-type oblong fryer, usually heated with H-shaped gas burners, is ideal. I also use an oblong fryer designed to work across two burners of my kitchen stove.

> 2 trout about 12 inches long
> 2 carrots, sliced
> ½ green bell pepper, sliced
> ½ red bell pepper, sliced
> 3 green onions, chopped with part of tops
> 2 slices canned pineapple
> ½ cup chicken stock
> ½ cup vinegar
> ½ cup sugar
> ½ cup flour
> 1 tablespoon cornstarch
> peanut oil (about 1 gallon for large deep fryer)
> salt and pepper

Rig for deep frying, and heat the oil to at least 375 degrees. While the oil is heating, cut the pineapple slices into wedges. In a saucepan, mix the carrots, green onions, pineapple, sugar, vinegar, chicken stock, and a little salt. (Hold the peppers until later.) Bring the mixture to a boil, turn the heat to low, and simmer for 15 minutes. Then add the cornstarch mixed with a little water, cooking and stirring until the sauce thickens. Keep the sauce warm.

Dry the dressed fish with a paper towel. Score the fish 3 times diagonally on each side. Sprinkle inside and out with salt and pepper, then roll in flour to coat both sides. Put the fish very carefully into the hot oil, and fry until nicely browned. The fish will float to the top when they are done, if you are using enough oil. Carefully remove the fish, and drain on brown paper.

Quickly heat the sauce almost to a boil. Add the peppers, stirring and cooking for 1 minute. Put each fish onto a separate plate, and pour the sauce over them. Serve hot with plenty of rice. This recipe is intended to serve 2 people, with the sauce spread evenly over 2 fish. If you have more people to serve, it's best to increase the measures accordingly and have a fish for each person. The Chinese often serve a larger fish in the middle of the table, and each person reaches out and helps himself with chopsticks. Most Americans do better with individual fish and a fork.

Note: This recipe was adapted from Jim Lee's *Chinese Cookbook,* and a longer version is used in my *Bass Cookbook.*

Hot-Stuff Trout

Some of my friends like to add hot pepper sauce to fried fish, and the stuff goes nicely with deep-fried trout. Some of them "marinate" the trout by sprinkling on a few drops of hot sauce and letting the fish sit for a couple of hours. Most of these hot sauces (such as Tabasco) have a red color, but some, such as jalapeño sauce, come in other colors. If you are into hot stuff, you will want to try some of the Mexican and Caribbean sauces. The hottest stuff I have ever tasted was given to me by a fellow named Fred Cutchens, who made it from his own garden. I don't know how he made it, but it was a mistake to put a little on your finger and touch your tongue to it. A local joke has it that 2 drops will unstop clogged plumbing. Anyhow, after "marinating" the trout with a few drops of hot sauce, it is dusted with cornmeal or other coating and fried as usual.

Another method is to add some cayenne pepper to the cornmeal or flour used to coat the fish. Then the fish is fried as usual. This method works better than trying to sprinkle cayenne over individual fish, if you have mixed the pepper and the cornmeal thoroughly. I don't have exact measures for either the cornmeal or the cayenne. If in doubt, start with 1 tablespoon of cayenne per cup of cornmeal. Dust a fish with the mixture, fry it, and take a test bite. If it is too hot for you, add more cornmeal. If it isn't hot enough, add more cayenne. Dried red pepper flakes can be used instead of packaged cayenne, but they should be ground into a powder in your mortar and pestle. Wash your hands after handling this stuff.

THREE

Trout on the Grill

Grilling a trout over hot wood coals provides excellent eating, and it seems to satisfy a faint primitive yearning in man. These days, grilling can also be accomplished quite successfully over gas-heated lava rocks or electric heat. Although grilling seems at first to be very close to broiling (cooking under the heat), there is a difference. Grilling is more of a hands-on kind of cooking, where the cook stands over and watches the process as he goes. Perhaps more important is the fact that smoke rises from the heat, either from wood or wood chips or from drippings from the fish or the basting liquid. The smoke adds flavor and aroma, and the drippings add sizzle.

Although the arena for grilling is still pretty much the patio, the same techniques and most of the same recipes can be used in camp or in the kitchen. That's right. A number of modern grills can be used indoors, and I am very fond of using the built-in grill on my electric stove. It's very handy day or night, rain or shine.

In my opinion, all true grilling is done on a rack over an open fire or coals. This includes cooking on a spit or kabob skewer. In this chapter I also include cooking on a grill with a hood that covers the fish or meat. The hoods come in handy for adding more smoke to the flavor, or for cooking large fish by the indirect method—that is, by using a large grill with a covered hood and putting the fire in one section and the fish in the other. This can be compared to cooking in an oven with the advantage of some smoke for flavor.

In direct grilling, the rule of thumb is that the smaller the fish, the closer it should be to the heat, within reason. The larger

28

the fish, the farther away it should be from the heat. In both cases, the idea is to get the inside done at the exact time the outside is nicely browned. It's not hard, but it requires constant attention and some common sense. Actually, each time you grill fish is a new experience in cooking. In any case, here are some tips to consider.

1. Use good fuel. If you use charcoal, consider getting the real stuff instead of using briquettes. It's more expensive, but it burns better and gets hotter. Also, it isn't stuck together with additives. If you use briquettes, it's best to avoid the self-starting kind, which contain even more additives. I'll admit to using the liquid starting fluid from time to time, and I find it very handy to have, but I really prefer to start a fire with the aid of twigs, paper, or some such kindling.

If you've got the time, consider building a hardwood fire and letting it burn down to coals. Green wood, although hard to start burning, makes good coals and provides wonderful smoke. When grilling for a large crowd, consider using hard coal instead of charcoal, if you can find it these days. Coal burns long and hot.

2. Let your fire get hot. Always allow plenty of time for your fire to get hot, be it wood, charcoal, briquettes, gas-heated larva rocks, or an electric coil and grate. My stove-top unit, which has an electric coil over a cast-iron grate, requires 30 minutes to get at its best.

3. Grease your rack. I like to grease my grilling rack before building the fire, then again just before I put the fish or meat on for cooking. Bacon grease is my favorite, but any good cooking oil will do. A new rack should be greased and heated a time or two over a hot fire to break it in and season it.

4. Spare the wire brush. My wife says that my opinion on this step is wishful thinking, but I like to think that failure to clean the grate after grilling on it prevents rust and promotes seasoning.

5. Baste—but not too much. Although most trout are on the oily side and therefore don't require as much basting as a walleye or such fish with dry, white flesh, a good basting with oil or butter will help keep the surface moist and aid in browning. A little oil on the surface of the fish also helps it absorb last-minute additions of salt and pepper and perhaps herbs. Be warned, however, that basting can be overdone, especially with thick tomato-based sauces, which tend to burn if applied too early during the grilling process.

6. *Get gear that works.* The price of a piece of grilling gear does not necessarily indicate how useful it will be to you. Spatulas are especially useful to me for grilling fish; in fact, I like to have two spatulas when turning fillets, one for the bottom and one for the top. But the metal in some spatulas is far too thick. You need a thin spatula, made of what I call "spring steel." This will help you get under the fish without tearing it. Also, I prefer spatulas of normal kitchen length instead of the long-handled variety sold for patio cooking.

7. *Use a grilling basket or rig one.* If you grill lots of fish, you might consider getting a hinged grilling basket. I highly recommend the adjustable rectangular models, which can hold small whole fish or thin fillets. Kabob baskets are also available, and there is even a fish-shaped basket for holding whole large fish. Using a basket, of course, facilitates turning the fish without tearing it.

You can easily rig a sort of grilling basket with two wire racks of equal size. Merely putting the fish on one rack and putting the other rack on top when you are ready to turn the fish will work nicely, if you can make the turn without getting burned. Asbestos gloves will help.

8. *Watch your business.* Unless you are cooking a large fish by the indirect method or are using some sort of combination smoker and cooker, grilling fish is a full-time job. Refuse to answer the telephone or do chores while you man the grill. It's just too easy to burn fish when you are cooking very close to hot coals. In addition to turning and basting the fish properly, you'll need to keep an eye peeled for flare-ups. That's why I often keep a cold beer in hand while grilling.

9. *Serve grilled fish hot.* Large fish cooked by the indirect method may take an hour or longer, but small fish and fillets can

be grilled in a matter of minutes. It is therefore sometimes best to have everything else ready to eat before you start grilling.

Most of the recipes in this chapter are geared toward charcoal or other patio cookers, as well as kitchen rigs. For campfire cooking, see chapter 8.

Grilled Whole Trout

Here's a recipe for grilling whole trout of about 1 pound each. It works best over medium hot coals with the rack about 6 inches above the heat. I like to use a rectangular grilling basket, if I've got one handy.

> 4 trout, about 1 pound each
> ¼ cup melted butter
> juice of 1 lemon
> ¼ teaspoon lemon zest
> 1 teaspoon chopped fresh rosemary
> Hungarian paprika
> salt and pepper
> lemon wedges for garnish

Mix a marinade with the melted butter, lemon juice, lemon zest, and rosemary. Put the fish into a suitable container, pour the marinade over them, and refrigerate for about 2 hours. Rig for grilling at medium heat. Grease a grilling basket or the rack of your grill. Salt and pepper the fish inside and out, then place them in the basket or on the grill and position 6 inches above the heat. Grill for 8 minutes on each side, basting from time to time with the marinade. Do not cook too long; the fish is done when it flakes easily when tested with a fork. Sprinkle a little paprika over the fish and serve, garnishing with lemon wedges.

Note: If you don't have fresh rosemary on hand, use ½ teaspoon dried.

Grilled Trout with Roe

Fish roe is one of my favorite foods. Here's an excellent way to make use of a small amount of roe. First poach it whole for 10 minutes in salted water, then break the sac and mash up the eggs. For the measures below, you'll need about 1 tablespoon of roe. You can double or otherwise adjust the measures. Any poached roe that you have left over can be refrigerated and scrambled with some chicken eggs for breakfast, served with a slice or two of bacon.

> small trout
> ½ cup butter
> 1 tablespoon poached roe
> 1 tablespoon minced fresh parsley
> juice of ½ lemon
> salt and pepper

Melt the butter, then stir in the roe, parsley, lemon juice, salt, and pepper. Keep warm. Sprinkle the trout inside and out with salt and pepper, then grill it on both sides until nicely done. Place the trout onto a heated serving platter and spoon on some of the roe butter.

Variations: Use lobster tomalley (liver) instead of fish roe. Commercial caviar can also be used, but most of this will be on the salty side, so adjust your seasonings accordingly.

Grilled Lake Trout Wheels

Here's a good method of grilling a lake trout or other rather large trout. Start a fire in the grill, and grease the rack. Skin and fillet the fish so that you have boneless slabs. Cut each fillet crosswise into strips exactly 1 inch wide. Dip the strips into a mixture of melted butter (or margarine) and lemon juice, then sprinkle with salt and pepper. Roll the strips into wheels, and pin them with toothpicks. Grill about 4 inches above hot wood coals. Baste once or twice with melted butter or margarine and lemon juice. Cook for 10 minutes, turning once with tongs.

Variations: Before rolling the strips into wheels, sprinkle them with chopped parsley or watercress, or with a little basil.

Hot Grilled Brook Trout

Here's a good recipe that I got from a booklet published by the McIlhenny Company, the Tabasco sauce people. If you like hot stuff, be sure to try it.

 4 brook trout, about 1 pound each
 ¼ cup fresh lemon juice
 2 tablespoons melted butter
 2 tablespoons olive oil
 2 tablespoons sesame seeds
 2 tablespoons chopped fresh parsley
 1 tablespoon Tabasco sauce
 ½ teaspoon ground ginger
 ½ teaspoon salt

Pierce the skin of each trout several times with a fork. Mix the rest of the ingredients, and coat the fish inside and out. Refrigerate for about 1 hour. Grill the trout about 5 inches from hot coals. Turn and grill for another 5 minutes, or until the fish flakes easily when tested with a fork.

Marinated Grilled Trout

Here's a recipe that I like to cook on my stove-top grill. Either fillets or whole small trout can be used.

 1 to 2 pounds trout fillets
 ½ cup olive oil
 ¼ cup dry white wine
 ¼ cup white wine vinegar
 1 medium onion, chopped
 1 tablespoon chopped fresh thyme
 salt

Prepare the trout and put them into a nonmetallic bowl. Mix the rest of the ingredients together and pour over the trout, tossing to coat all sides. Refrigerate for 2 hours or a little longer. Heat the grill, and grease the rack. Grill the trout, basting from time to time with the marinade, for 4 or 5 minutes on each side, or until the meat flakes easily when tested with a fork. (Large trout or thick fillets will take longer.) When the fish are almost done, sprinkle on a little salt to taste.

Note: Some people object to basting with leftover marinade. If you wish, you can make a little extra marinade and save it separately as a basting sauce.

Trout Kabobs

Fish kabobs can be a little tricky unless the fish has a firm flesh, such as swordfish. The problem is that the fish chunks tear during handling, or else they don't turn properly. It helps to make a special kabob rig in which the fish won't be in direct contact with a grill. This precludes sticking and works better in every way, it seems to me. In order to do this, merely place some bricks on either side of the coals, making two parallel rows of suitable distance apart and of a suitable height. Rest the ends of the skewers on the bricks, with the fish chunks directly over the fire. (I have also seen special grills made for holding skewers in this manner; usually, they are shaped like a rectangular box without a top or bottom and with skewer slots or notches on opposite sides.)

For fish kabobs, I usually like to use two wooden skewers in tandem instead of a single skewer. Wooden bamboo skewers are inexpensive and can be reused if they are soaked in water to prevent them from burning.

Any good heat source can be used, but I prefer wood coals or pure charcoal. Hard coal is also good and burns a long time. Use soaked wood chips, or green wood, if you want some smoke.

This recipe calls for fruit, but you can use vegetables or just plain fish if you prefer.

The Kabobs
1 or 2 pounds trout fillets
large seedless grapes
fresh pineapple cut into 1½-inch chunks

The Marinade
½ cup peanut oil
¼ cup fresh orange juice
2 tablespoons soy sauce
1 tablespoon onion juice
2 tablespoons chopped green onions with tops
2 tablespoons chopped fresh parsley
2 teaspoons orange zest
salt and pepper

Cut the fillets into 1½-inch chunks, and put them into a non-metallic bowl. Mix the marinade ingredients, and pour over the trout chunks, tossing to mix well. Refrigerate for 1 hour. Rig for grilling. When the coals are ready, cover the skewers with oil and thread on the fish, alternating with grapes and chunks of pineapple. Grill about 4 inches from the heat for 3 minutes. Turn and baste with the leftover marinade. Grill for another 3 minutes. Turn and baste. Grill for another 2 minutes on each side, basting with each turn. Test for doneness. Serve hot with rice or pilaf and vegetables.

Shashlik of Trout

The Russians are especially fond of fresh fish, and, of course, everyone knows of their love of caviar. They also claim to have invented the kabob—but the Turks contest this hotly. In any case, here's a very attractive Russian dish, as well as a tasty one. It's best to cook it, like any kabob, over charcoal or wood coals, but gas or electric grills also work nicely. The kabobs can also be broiled quite successfully. Use boneless and skinless fillets for this dish.

1 pound trout fillet, boned and skinned
1 pound fresh mushroom caps
½ pint sour cream
¼ pound red caviar
juice of 1 lemon
dry bread crumbs
butter
salt and pepper
boiled new potatoes (cooked separately)

Prepare the grill or broiler. Cut the trout fillet into kabob-size chunks, baste them with melted butter, sprinkle them with salt and pepper, roll them in bread crumbs, and put them onto skewers, alternating with mushroom caps. Sprinkle the kabobs lightly with lemon juice, and grill about 6 inches above the heat until the meat is done. (Usually, 10 minutes per inch of thickness will be about right, turning once.) While the kabobs grill, sauté the rest of the mushrooms in a little butter. Combine the sour cream and red caviar. Serve the kabobs very hot, along with the sautéed mushrooms, the sour cream and caviar mixture, and the boiled new potatoes.

Sesame Trout

This dish can be cooked over charcoal, electric, or gas heat, or over wood coals. It's best to put the fish into a hinged grilling basket so that they can be turned easily. The sesame seeds work best, I think, with quick grilling over high heat; for that reason, use small trout, 9 or 10 inches long.

6 to 8 small trout
1 cup butter
¼ cup sesame seeds
juice of 2 lemons
1 tablespoon salt
¼ teaspoon black pepper

Gut the fish and wash them under running water. Put the fish into a shallow nonmetallic pan or zip-closure bag. Mix the lemon juice, salt, and pepper, then pour the mixture over the trout, turning to coat all sides. Refrigerate for several hours. Turn the fish (or the bag) from time to time.

Rig for grilling. While the coals get ready, toast the sesame seeds in a small skillet, shaking the pan constantly, until the seeds are golden. Add the butter, and stir until it melts. Keep warm. Fit the fish into a grilling basket and lock shut. Baste both sides with the sesame seed butter. Grill the fish close to the heat for 4 or 5 minutes on each side, basting a couple of times.

Variation: The fish can also be broiled.

Trout Teriyaki

This delicious dish can be cooked in camp, on the patio, or on the kitchen grill. It's best to use only small fish (no more than 9 inches) and 2 skewers (metal or wooden) so that the fish can be turned over. I skewer 2 or more fish together, depending on how many I've got to cook. It's best to leave the heads on the fish, gut them, and lay them on their sides for skewering. Run parallel skewers through the cavity opening and out the top, thereby making the fish lie flat on the grill. (If you are cooking in camp, you can use small green sticks as skewers.) It's best to soak dried bamboo or other wooden skewers in water before using them.

> small trout
> ½ cup sake or dry vermouth
> ½ cup soy sauce
> 1 tablespoon olive oil
> juice of 1 lemon
> 2 cloves garlic, crushed
> 1 teaspoon brown sugar

Mix the sake, soy sauce, olive oil, lemon juice, garlic, and brown sugar. Draw the fish, wash them, and place them in a non-metallic container. Pour the marinade over the fish, tossing to coat all sides. Marinate for an hour in the refrigerator. Rig for grilling, and skewer the fish as directed above. Grill over a hot fire for 3 or 4 minutes on each side, basting 2 or 3 times with the leftover marinade.

Variations: Add a little grated fresh ginger root to the marinade. Substitute sesame oil for the olive oil.

A Trout Recipe for the Amazin' Man

In a letter to Duncan Barnes, editor of *Field & Stream* magazine, an Englishman by the name of Brian Hewitt said that he had read an article on lure making by A. D. Livingston and that he needed to get in touch with this "amazin' man." The fellow said that he had purchased a copy of my *Luremaking* book, which dealt mostly with leadheads. What he sorely needed, however, was some information about making plugs and soft plastic lures. I answered the fellow's letter as best I could. After squirming a little with the plugs and soft plastic questions, I told him that I was doing a book on trout cookery, and I wondered whether he might have a strictly British recipe or two for me.

He wrote back that he is a holographic engineer and has plans for manufacturing a flutter spoon with "this amazin' material." He sent me a sample, and I'll allow that it looks very good and has a flash like no other. He also sent me a copy of an article called "The Use of Holographic Material as an Attracting Bait," published in *Pikelines,* a British publication. And, yes, he did indeed have recipes.

The trout, he said, is usually filleted and grilled over charcoal. "It is prepared with a herb we call rosemary, a little lemon juice, and some garlic, and is served with a pasta side dish, peppered, perhaps 'egged' (i.e., you drop an egg into a just-out-of-the-saucepan cooked plain pasta dish and mix, cooking the egg into the pasta and serving real quick). Served with cold white wine. . . . It's amazin'."

Indeed it is.

Grilled Trout with Herb Butter

This recipe works best with small trout about 9 inches long. Using a hinged grill basket is recommended.

>   4 to 8 small trout
>   ½ cup soft butter
>   juice of 1 large lemon
>   6 green onions, chopped with part of tops
>   2 tablespoons chopped fresh parsley
>   ½ teaspoon basil
>   ½ teaspoon chervil
>   ⅛ teaspoon tarragon
>   ¼ teaspoon cayenne
>   salt and pepper

Rig for grilling over charcoal, or use a gas or electric grill. Place the rack about 4 inches above the heat source, and grease a hinged basket if you have one. Salt and pepper the trout cavities. Mix the other ingredients and brush both sides of the trout. Grill the trout, turning and basting every 2 minutes, for a total of 10 minutes. When done, the fish will flake easily when tested with a fork and the flesh will be opaque. Serve hot.

FOUR

Trout in the Oven

Trout bake remarkably well either whole or filleted, as well as in casseroles. The flesh of trout is on the oily side, which helps prevent it from drying out while baking. Most trout can be baked as is, but some large fish may be excessively fatty, in which case the belly flab should be trimmed off.

Although fatty fish don't dry out as badly as lean fish, it is still very important that the trout not be baked too long. It's always best to follow the recipe closely, but keep in mind that the rule of thumb for cooking fish is 10 minutes per inch of thickness. I usually allow a little more time, however, if the fish is put into the oven in a cold baking pan or dish. Also, stuffed fish will require a longer cooking time, usually an extra 10 minutes.

For perfect baking, it is important that you know your oven. These days, some of the more expensive ovens have options, such as forced air circulation, that may alter the cooking times significantly and may cause the outside of the fish to get brown before the inside is done. I prefer a large oven with regular heat coming from the bottom. If I have a choice, I'll use electric ovens. (I've always said that the ideal stove would have 2 electric ovens, 4 stove-top gas burners, a powerful blowtorch-type gas burner for heating the bottom of a large wok, and a large electric grilling unit, also suitable for deep fryers, with a strong downdraft suction fan.) If you use a convected air oven (that is, an oven with forced air circulation), be sure to read the manufacturer's instructions.

Broiling is a separate cooking operation in which the heat comes from the top; this is covered in chapter 5.

Cooking in a microwave oven is an entirely different ball game, and the instruction book for your unit should be followed to the letter. Cooking times will vary drastically from those set forth in my baking recipes in this chapter. Conversions can be made, but I don't recommend this practice. If you are going to use a microwave as a primary cooking device, it's best to build the recipes from scratch. One problem with microwaving fish is that part of the fish may get overcooked while another part may remain raw. I can see the advantages to quick cooking, especially the quick reheating of previously cooked foods, but I really don't enjoy microwave cooking and seldom do it. There are other opinions, however, and I would like to refer the reader to Paula J. Del Giudice's *Microwave Game & Fish Cookbook,* published by Stackpole Books. To get you started, a recipe adapted from this book appears toward the end of this chapter.

I also include a recipe for Oven-Fried Fish, although I don't like this term simply because the fish isn't fried. I'm not going to argue with the results, however. Also, some baking recipes call for putting the fish into a baking bag or encasing it in brown paper. These fish are more steamed than baked, but, again, I'm not going to argue with the results.

In any case, here are some tips to help you cook better trout in your oven.

1. Bake in the center. The temperature in an oven varies quite a bit from one spot to another. A baking dish on the very bottom can be influenced by radiant heat, and the very top of the oven is also hotter because heat rises. The middle is more dependable. Adjust the oven racks so that the fish will be in the middle.

2. Test the accuracy of your thermostat. Put an oven thermometer in the center of your oven, and test it against your thermostat setting. After making this test a few times, allow for any variation when setting the oven temperature.

3. Grease your baking pan. Although fatty fish don't stick to the bottom of a pan as badly as lean fish, it's always better to grease your pan with at least a light coating of oil or with a cooking spray.

4. Use a meat thermometer on large fish. Although I don't recommend it, many anglers like to put a large trout on the table whole. Baking a whole trout can be a little tricky, and it's best to insert a meat thermometer into the thickest part of the fish. Start the thermometer in near the head and insert it at an angle, going back toward the tail. Do not touch the rib cage or backbone. The fish is done when the thermometer reads between 140 and 145 degrees.

5. Baste with pan juices. Basting the fish from time to time helps it to brown. But don't overdo it; opening the oven lets out lots of heat and may delay the cooking. When you do baste, be quick about it.

6. Leave the head, tail, and skin on baked fish. These parts will help hold in the juices, especially at the head end. The head also makes very good eating if gnawing and nibbling are permitted at the table. If you must remove the head and tail for the benefit of squeamish guests, leave them on the fish during the baking process and remove them before serving. I usually cook the trout with the skin on and remove it before serving.

7. Garnish. Add color as well as flavor to whole baked fish by serving with freshly sliced lemon, parsley, or some such garnish.

8. Bake in a serving pan. If you have a baking pan suitable for serving, use it. This will minimize handling the fish and will send the fish to the table with all the good pan juices. If you want a quaint touch in addition to providing some fine eating, bake a large trout on a greased oak plank. Actually, any good hardwood plank of suitable size can be used, but it should be rather thick. To go whole hog with this technique, surround the cooked fish with a dam of fluffy white mashed potatoes, and put some green peas and other colorful vegetables between the baked fish and the potatoes.

9. Preheat the oven. Always heat the oven for about 20 minutes before baking your fish. Some electric ovens have a special setting for preheating that turns on both the broiler and the bottom heating unit; before cooking, be sure to switch the setting to bake.

10. Don't overcook. Cooking a trout in a dry oven for too long is one of the worst things you can do to it. Use your timer.

Baked Trout Paprika

When used in sufficient quantities, paprika adds color as well as flavor to fish and other foods. While it is ideal for white-fleshed fish, such as cod, it can also be used to advantage in cooking those trout whose flesh is not a pronounced reddish or pink color. There are several kinds of paprika. Most of the Hungarian imports are quite mild, but the Spanish and Portuguese paprikas are generally on the hot side and vary widely from one brand to another. It you wish to add color, lots of the mild kind obviously works better than a pinch of the hot kind.

> 2 pounds trout fillets
> 2 medium tomatoes, sliced
> 1 medium onion, diced
> 1 large green bell pepper, diced
> juice of 1 lemon
> ¼ cup butter
> salt and pepper
> paprika
> ½ tablespoon finely chopped fresh dill for garnish

Sprinkle the fish with freshly squeezed lemon juice, and set aside for 30 minutes. Preheat the oven to 350 degrees. Melt the butter in a small skillet, and sauté the onion and green pepper for 5 minutes. Add the tomatoes, and simmer for 10 minutes, stirring in the paprika. Grease a casserole dish of suitable size, and place the fish on the bottom; the fish should fit snugly without overlapping. Sprinkle the trout with salt and pepper, pour in the sauce, and smooth out. Bake for 20 minutes, or until the flesh flakes easily when tested with a fork. Sprinkle lightly with dill before serving.

Note: If you've got other sorts of fresh peppers in the garden, try them instead of the bell pepper. I often grow mild banana peppers and find that they go nicely in this dish. Go easy on hot peppers, however.

Stuffed Large Trout

This recipe works best for trout of 8 to 10 pounds, baked with the head and tail on. If the fish is very fat, it's best to trim the belly.

1 large trout, 8 to 10 pounds
2½ cups soft bread crumbs
1 rib celery with green tops, diced
1 medium onion, diced
½ cup sour cream
3 tablespoons butter, divided
melted butter for basting
juice of 1 lemon for basting
zest from lemon rind
½ teaspoon salt
½ teaspoon paprika

Preheat the oven to 400 degrees. Wash and dry the fish, then sprinkle lemon juice inside the body cavity. To make a stuffing, sauté the onion and celery in 2 tablespoons butter for 5 or 6 minutes. Stir in the bread crumbs, sour cream, lemon zest, and a little salt. (To get the lemon zest, scrape or grate off the outer part of the lemon before squeezing out the juice, avoiding the bitter white pith. Use a lemon zester if you've got one.) Put the fish into a greased baking pan of suitable size. If you don't have a pan long enough for the fish, consider making a pan with about 3 thicknesses of extra-heavy aluminum foil. Remove the oven rack, put the foil on it, add the fish, and turn up the edges of the foil, making a boat. When you remove the fish from the oven, take out the entire rack and proceed carefully.

Stuff the fish loosely, leaving room for the stuffing to swell, then baste it with a mixture of lemon juice and 1 tablespoon melted butter. Truss the fish, or tie it about 3 times around the middle with cotton string in order to hold in the stuffing. (You can also sew up the fish with a needle and thread or use small skewers.) Sprinkle the fish with salt and paprika. Estimate or measure the thickness of the fish at the widest part. Bake in the preheated oven for 10 minutes per inch of thickness plus another 10 minutes for the stuffing. Baste lightly 2 or 3 times while the trout is cooking.

To check the fish for doneness, you can cut into the thickest part. If the flesh is opaque, it's done; if not, cook the fish a little longer. You also can use a meat thermometer on a large fish, following the directions under tip 4 at the beginning of this chapter.

Baked Trout Sierra Madre

I don't know the history of this recipe, which I have adapted it from *Game and Fish Cookbook*, by Harriet and James Barnett, who used several recipes that called for dipping the fish in salted milk. They also deal in pinches of some of the ingredients, which, I suppose, indicates an amount that is easily taken between thumb and forefinger. (Use a sparing pinch of the cayenne, which is very hot.) This recipe can be used to cook a whole fish, but I prefer boneless fillets.

> 3 pounds trout fillets
> ½ cup milk
> 2 tomatoes, skinned and thinly sliced
> 1 medium onion, thinly sliced
> 1 cup mushrooms, thinly sliced
> 6 tablespoons butter
> 6 tablespoons soft bread crumbs
> 4 tablespoons sherry
> 1 tablespoon chopped parsley
> ¼ teaspoon salt
> pinch nutmeg
> pinch fennel
> pinch cayenne
> 2 or 3 pinches white pepper

Preheat the oven to 450 degrees. Stir the salt into the milk, and pour over the fish. Melt the butter in a baking dish, coating all sides. Flop the fillets around in the butter, then take them out.

45

Put the bread crumbs into the pan, stir them about to coat with butter, and remove them with a spoon. Line the bottom of the dish with a layer of onion. Mix a little white pepper, cayenne, nutmeg, and fennel. Place the fish fillets into the baking dish, and sprinkle lightly with the spices. Add a layer of mushrooms, and top with a layer of tomatoes. Pour the sherry over the dish, then sprinkle with the buttered bread crumbs and chopped parsley. Bake uncovered at 450 degrees for 15 minutes. Whole fish usually takes a little longer; the fish is done when it flakes easily when tested with a fork.

Baked Trout with Spanish Sauce

I have never understood why sauces made with tomatoes and green peppers are called Spanish or Portuguese instead of American. In any case, this sauce is especially good when made with garden-fresh ingredients and served over baked fish. I usually make the sauce while the trout are cooking. Small whole trout can be used, but I prefer boneless fillets with any thick sauce.

The Fish
2 pounds boneless trout fillets
olive oil
milk
1 cup dry bread crumbs
olive oil
½ teaspoon salt
¼ teaspoon pepper

Preheat the oven to 350 degrees. Mix the salt and pepper into the bread crumbs. Flop the fillets in a little milk, then coat them with bread crumbs. Arrange the fillets in a greased baking dish, and brush with olive oil. Put the baking dish into the hot oven and cook for 20 to 25 minutes, or until the fish flakes easily when tested with a fork. The exact cooking time will depend on the thickness of the fish. While the fish cooks, make the sauce.

Spanish Sauce
4 medium tomatoes, peeled and diced
1 medium onion, diced
1 green bell pepper, diced
2 cloves garlic, minced
4 tablespoons olive oil
1 teaspoon salt
½ teaspoon black pepper
¼ cup flour
⅓ cup water

Mix a paste with ¼ cup flour and ⅓ cup water; set aside. Heat the olive oil in a skillet, and sauté the onions, green pepper, and garlic for 5 minutes. Add the tomatoes, salt, and pepper. Stir in the flour paste. Simmer for 30 minutes, stirring from time to time. Ideally, the sauce and the fish will be ready at the same time. Serve the sauce over the fish.

Easy Baked Trout

Here's a dish that is easy to prepare and is bound to be a hit. It can be cooked with whole trout, but I prefer boneless fillets. Be sure to try this one with fillets from a 5-pound lake trout.

2 or 3 pounds trout fillets
1 cup sour cream
1 medium onion, grated
½ teaspoon powdered mustard
salt and pepper
paprika

Preheat the oven to 400 degrees. Grease a covered baking pan or dish of suitable size to hold the fillets snugly without much overlapping. Salt and pepper the fillets, then place them skin side down in the baking dish. Cover and bake for 20 minutes. While waiting, mix the sour cream, grated onion, and mustard. After 20 minutes, preheat the broiler. Spread the sour cream mix-

47

ture over the fish, then sprinkle lightly with paprika. Broil until the fish brown on top and flake easily when tested with a fork. Remove the fillets carefully with a spatula.

Easy Baked Trout with Bacon

Here's an easy dish to prepare in the oven. I prefer to use very thin smoked bacon, so that not too much grease accumulates on the bottom of the dish.

> 4 to 6 small trout, heads on
> 8 to 12 strips thin bacon
> celery salt
> lemon wedges

Preheat the oven to 400 degrees. Find a baking dish that holds the trout snugly, then grease it with a strip of bacon. After heating a skillet, cook the bacon on low heat until it is about half done. Lightly sprinkle the trout inside and out with celery salt. Place the bacon across the top of the trout, crosswise, then put the baking pan in the center of the oven. Cook uncovered for 20 minutes. If the bacon is not quite crisp, turn on the broiler and cook a little longer, until the bacon looks ready to eat. Garnish with lemon wedges.

Easy Trout en Papillote

Fancy restaurants cook fish in oiled paper, folded over and sealed. It's easier to use aluminum foil, provided that no fish bones puncture the package. With a small trout, use extra-large heavy-duty aluminum foil, folding one end of the foil over the trout. Square up the edges. Make a fold all around with at least 1 inch of foil, then make another fold of about ½ inch, creating a double seal.

whole small trout
1 tablespoon butter
½ cup condensed cream of mushroom soup
parsley
salt and pepper

Place the butter inside the trout, along with a little salt and pepper. Place the fish on a sheet of aluminum foil, and cover with mushroom soup. Roll to coat all sides. Sprinkle lightly with parsley, salt, and pepper. Seal the foil, and put the package into the oven for 20 minutes—and hope it's done when you unpackage it. If in doubt, let it sit for a few minutes before you open the foil.

Note: You can use this recipe for cooking in camp. If necessary, put the foil directly onto a bed of hot coals. Turn the package after about 10 minutes, being careful not to puncture the foil. If available, substitute watercress for the parsley.

Easy Trout Fillets Piquant

This easy recipe makes a delicious dish. It's best to use boneless, skinless fillets about ½ inch thick. If you have large fish, cut the fillets crosswise into ½-inch-thick fingers.

1 pound trout fillets
dry bread crumbs
½ cup melted butter
1 tablespoon white wine vinegar
1 tablespoon white wine Worcestershire sauce
juice of 1 lemon or lime
1 teaspoon prepared mustard
salt and pepper
paprika

Preheat the oven to 450 degrees. Grease a suitable baking dish rather heavily with part of the butter. Cover the bottom of the dish with ¹⁄₁₆ to ⅛ inch of bread crumbs. Arrange the fillets on top of the bread crumbs without overlapping, if possible. Mix

49

what's left of the butter with the other ingredients, except for the paprika, and pour the mixture over the fillets. Bake in the center of the oven for 15 minutes. Sprinkle the fillets with paprika and cook for another minute or so, or until the flesh flakes easily when tested with a fork.

Irish Trout

This old Irish dish calls for wrapping a boned fish in a piece of "greaseproof" paper. I have cooked it with rainbows wrapped in a brown grocery bag and find the recipe to be better than New Orleans *Pompano en Papillates*. I read recently, however, that brown grocery bags made from recycled paper are not chemically safe for cooking and could catch on fire. I have never had a problem, but you may choose to use brown parchment paper made for cooking, if you can find it these days.

The recipe calls for shallots, which are now available in most supermarkets; if you can't find them, use small onions. The measures below are for a single trout of middling size. Cook several if you need them.

> 1 trout, about 1½ pounds
> ¼ cup butter
> 8 shallots
> 1 lemon
> 1 tablespoon chopped fresh chives
> 1 tablespoon chopped fresh parsley
> 1 teaspoon chopped fresh basil
> salt and pepper

Preheat the oven to 350 degrees. Clean the trout, then salt and pepper it inside and out. (My Irish recipe says to bone the trout, but I'm not going quite that far.) Grate the lemon rind carefully, getting the zest but not the bitter white inner pith. Then juice the lemon and remove the seeds. Peel and chop the shallots. Melt the butter in a small saucepan, then mix in the shallots, parsley, chives, basil, lemon zest, and lemon juice, along with a little

50

salt and pepper. Stuff the trout with this mixture, then wrap it with the parchment paper or brown grocery bag, making sure that you have at least 2 thicknesses. Tie the ends or fold them tightly. Carefully place the fish on a baking sheet or shallow pan. Bake in the center of the preheated oven for 20 minutes. Before removing the fish from the paper, make sure that the flesh flakes easily when tested with a fork; if not, put it back into the hot oven for a few more minutes.

Dakota Trout

Here's a good dish from South Dakota. The recipe was first published in *Cooking the Sportsman's Harvest,* by the South Dakota Department of Game, Fish, and Parks, and I present it in thinly disguised format. The original called for a dressed trout and said that the recipe was a good one for a large trout. How large? Try 5 pounds. Just remember that the ideal cooking time will vary with the thickness of the fish. The general rule is to cook it 10 minutes per inch of thickness, but in some cases this isn't quite enough, especially if the fish is stuffed. A better rule for a large fish, I think, is to cook it 20 minutes in a preheated oven for the first inch of thickness, and then allow 10 more minutes for each additional inch.

> whole dressed trout, about 5 pounds
> 1½ cups sour cream
> 1 cup chopped onion
> juice of 3 lemons
> 1 tablespoon Worcestershire sauce
> 1 tablespoon prepared mustard
> salt and pepper

Preheat the oven to 350 degrees. Line a pan of suitable size with aluminum foil. Sprinkle the trout inside and out with salt and pepper, then center it lengthwise on the aluminum foil. Mix the sour cream, onion, mustard, lemon juice, and Worcestershire sauce. Put about half of this mixture into the fish's body cavity, then pour the rest over the fish, bending up the aluminum foil a little all around to contain the sauce. Bake for 30 minutes or until the fish is done. Toward the end of the cooking period, baste with pan juice and test with a fork every 5 minutes, until the fish flakes easily.

Trout and Tomatoes

Here's a dish to try when you've got ripe tomatoes in the garden. It can be cooked with fillets, but it's best with small whole trout.

> small whole trout or fillets
> tomatoes, sliced
> butter
> onions, sliced
> salt

Preheat the oven to 400 degrees. Melt a little butter in a skillet, and sauté the onion slices for a few minutes. Sprinkle the trout inside and out with salt, and place in a greased baking dish. Place a slice of sautéed onion on the thick part of each trout, then arrange slices of tomatoes from one end to the other. Bake for 30 minutes, or until the fish flakes easily when tested with a fork.

Variations: Sprinkle a little grated cheese over the tomatoes. Also, try placing a strip of thin-sliced bacon over the tomatoes.

Lake Trout Louise

I don't know the origin of this recipe, which I have adapted from Sylvia Bashline's *The Bounty of the Earth Cookbook.* I cook it with low-fat yogurt whenever my wife goes on another diet.

4 lake trout fillets, about 2 pounds total
1 cup plain yogurt (low-fat if preferred)
1 tablespoon wine vinegar
2 teaspoons Dijon mustard
1 teaspoon sugar
5 drops Tabasco sauce
salt and pepper

Preheat the oven to 400 degrees. Grease a baking dish. Combine the yogurt, vinegar, sugar, mustard, Tabasco sauce, salt, and pepper. Place the fillets in the baking dish, and spread the sauce mixture over them. Bake in the center of the oven for 25 to 30 minutes, or until the fish flakes easily when tested with a fork.

Note: I have also cooked this recipe successfully with whole rainbow trout about 12 inches long.

Easy Trout Parmigiana

I make this dish with canned spaghetti sauce with mushrooms, but it can also be made with ordinary tomato sauce. The recipe calls for grated Parmesan cheese. For this it's best to use block Parmesan cheese and grate it yourself.

2 pounds trout fillets
1 cup canned spaghetti sauce
½ cup grated Parmesan cheese
salt and pepper
melted butter

Preheat the oven to 425 degrees. Grease a shallow baking dish of suitable size. Place the fish skin side down, and sprinkle with salt and pepper. Spread the spaghetti sauce evenly over the fillets, sprinkle with the grated Parmesan, and drizzle with melted butter. Bake uncovered for 15 to 20 minutes, or until the fish flakes easily when tested with a fork.

Trout Baked in Wine

This Brazilian dish makes a nice way to serve fish for a special occasion. It can be made with small trout (9 or 10 inches long) or with fillets from larger fish. It should be cooked in a baking dish just big enough to hold the trout without overlapping very much.

        4 to 6 small trout
        1 cup dry white wine
        4 tablespoons melted butter
        2 tablespoons dry bread crumbs
        4 tablespoons chopped green onions with tops
        2 tablespoons chopped fresh parsley
        2 cloves garlic, minced
        juice of 1 lemon
        salt and white pepper

Preheat the oven to 400 degrees. Pan-dress the trout (or fillet them if you are using large fish), and rub them inside and out with lemon juice. Then sprinkle the fish with salt and white pepper, and arrange them in a greased baking dish of suitable size. Sprinkle the minced garlic evenly over the trout, and pour on the wine. Mix the parsley, green onions, and bread crumbs; sprinkle evenly over the trout, then spoon on the melted butter, spreading it evenly. Bake uncovered in the center of the oven for 20 minutes, or until the fish flakes easily when tested with a fork. Do not overcook.

Trout Bercy

A bercy sauce is made from Fish Stock (or fumet), white wine, shallots, and other ingredients. It is sometimes used over poached fish, but I also like it in this baked trout version. Note that the bercy sauce below is a simplified form. If you've got plenty of time, consult a French cookbook. If not, try my easy version, call it Trout Bercy, and buy an extra bottle of that wine.

> 4 or 5 trout, 10 to 12 inches, dressed whole
> 1 cup Fish Stock (see chapter 13)
> 1 cup dry white wine
> ¼ cup butter
> ¼ cup chopped shallots
> salt and white pepper

In a saucepan, boil the Fish Stock until it is reduced by half. Add the wine. Preheat the oven to 325 degrees. Melt half of the butter in a shallow baking dish of suitable size. Pour in the chopped shallots, and spread them evenly over the bottom of the baking pan. Sprinkle the trout with salt and white pepper, then place them over the shallots. Pour the fish stock and wine mixture over the fish. Bake in the center of the oven for 15 or 20 minutes, or until the fish flakes easily when tested with a fork.

Trout Steaks Alaska

I don't know where this recipe originated, but I got it from a booklet published by the McIlhenny Company, the Tabasco sauce people of Avery Island, Louisiana, which is a long way from Alaska. But maybe the Tabasco folks reckoned that a drop or two of heat would be welcomed in the Far North. The original called for salmon steaks, but steaks from large trout can also be used and will respond well to Tabasco. Make the sauce while the fish is cooking.

The Fish
4 trout steaks, 1 inch thick
¼ cup butter
4½ teaspoons lemon or lime juice
¼ teaspoon Tabasco sauce
salt

Preheat the oven to 350 degrees. In a saucepan, melt the butter, and stir in the lemon or lime juice and Tabasco sauce. Lightly grease a shallow dish, and place the trout steaks in it. Sprinkle lightly with salt, then pour the butter sauce over the steaks. Bake for 25 minutes, or until the fish flakes easily when tested with a fork. Serve with the following sauce.

The Sauce
½ pint sour cream
1 cup diced cucumber
1 tablespoon snipped fresh dill
¼ teaspoon salt

Mix the sauce ingredients, and set aside. When the trout is done, top with the sauce.

Variation: Cook the steaks on the grill instead of in the oven. Mix a basting sauce with the melted butter, lemon or lime juice, Tabasco sauce, and salt. Marinate the steaks in this mixture for 1 hour, or at least until the charcoal gets hot, and grill as usual, basting several times. Do not overcook. With the grilled version, omit the cucumber sauce.

Togue Fillets with Sauce

Here's a dish from Maine, where lake trout are often called *togue*. Since the recipe calls for rather small fillets, any trout about 12 inches long can be used successfully. Start with skinless fillets, then flatten them slightly by pounding with a meat mallet. Roll each fillet, starting with the small end. Push in the top center of the roll, forming a pocket, and pin at the bottom with a round toothpick. Note that the recipe calls for a skillet with an oven-proof handle and a domed lid; use your stove-top Dutch oven if necessary.

> 4 lake trout (togue) fillets, rolled (see above)
> 1 cup heavy whipping cream
> 2 tablespoons butter
> 1 chicken egg yolk
> ½ cup dry white wine
> ½ cup finely chopped onion
> 4 ounces fresh mushrooms, chopped
> salt and pepper

Preheat the oven to 350 degrees. Heat 1 tablespoon butter in a small skillet or saucepan, then sauté the mushrooms until tender. In a 10-inch ovenproof skillet, melt the remaining butter and sauté the onions for 5 minutes. Arrange the rolled fillets on top of the onions, setting them with the cupped part up. Spoon the mushrooms into the cups. Sprinkle with salt and pepper. Pour the wine over the fish rolls, and heat on top of the stove to a boil. Cover the skillet and put it into the preheated oven for 10 minutes. Then remove the rolled fillets carefully with a spatula, and put them onto a hot serving platter.

Stir the cream into the skillet and heat to a boil, then reduce the heat and simmer until the sauce is reduced by a third. Remove the skillet from the heat. Put the egg yolk into a small bowl, then stir in a little of the sauce. Next, stir the egg yolk mixture into the contents of the skillet, adding a little salt and pepper. Bring to heat, but do not boil. Pour the sauce over the rolled togue fillets. Serve hot.

Microwaved Bernardied Brookies

At the outset of this chapter, I admitted that I am not an accomplished microwave cook and I referred the reader to Paula J. Del Giudice's *Microwave Game & Fish Cookbook*. Here's a recipe from that work.

"The origin of this recipe," the author says, "is a drink fondly called the Hot Bernardi. To those who've shared the Hot Bernardi, I hope you'll forgive the change in ingredients. Hot Bernardis are especially good after fishing for brook trout in your favorite neck of the woods."

    12 brook trout, pan-dressed
    4 tablespoons butter
    4 tablespoons concentrated orange juice
    ¼ medium onion, coarsely chopped
    3 tablespoons bourbon
    ½ orange, thinly sliced

Arrange the trout in a layer in an 8-inch square microwave-able baking dish, with the thickest parts of the fish facing the outside of the dish. In a small saucepan, microwave the butter and concentrated orange juice for 1 minute on high. Stir the onions and bourbon into the butter mixture. Pour this mixture over the trout. Cover. Microwave on 80 percent power for 5 minutes. Remove the cover, then spread the orange slices over the top of the fish. Cover again, and microwave on 80 percent power for another 5 minutes. Let the dish sit for several minutes before serving so that it will continue cooking.

Oven-Fried Trout

There are several coatings designed to make baked fish look like fried fish. Try Shake 'n Bake, for example, following the directions on the package. You can also easily come up with your own coating, or use the following:

    1 to 2 pounds trout fillets, about ½ inch thick
    flour
    fine bread crumbs
    1 chicken egg, whisked
    butter
    salt and pepper

Preheat the oven to 450 degrees. Grease a baking pan of suitable size with butter. Salt and pepper the fillets, then roll (or shake) them in flour, dip them in beaten chicken egg, roll them in bread crumbs, and arrange in a single layer in the baking pan. Drizzle some melted butter on top, and bake for 10 minutes, or until the fillets are nicely browned and flake easily when tested with a fork.

Note: Instead of drizzling on the butter, you can freeze a stick and then grate it over the fish. This method is less messy and distributes the butter evenly.

FIVE

Broiled Trout

Broiling fish under the heat, as distinguished from grilling it over the heat, is one of the better ways to cook trout fillets. The method is easy—but it's also exacting and not foolproof. The general rule is to cook the fish as close as possible to the heat without burning the surface before the inside gets done. Consequently, the thicker the fish, the farther it must be from the heat.

Thin fillets work better than whole fish, except that they are difficult to move without tearing. The good news is that thin fillets don't necessarily have to be turned. I often start the fillets cooking on a cast-iron griddle on top of the stove, and then put the whole works into the oven, thereby cooking both top and bottom. Small whole fish can be broiled successfully, but these have to be turned over. Most broiling pans have a rack across the top so that the fish juices and basting liquid are contained below. Some of these racks are wire, and some are sheet metal with slots. Fish tend to stick to either kind. If your hinged grilling rack fits under your broiler, use it for fish that have to be turned. Here are a few more tips on broiling trout.

1. *Choose the highest temperature setting.* On most modern electric kitchen stoves, the heat is controlled thermostatically. Unless you have reason to do otherwise, turn the setting to broil, or the highest heat. Then you can lower the rack with larger fish. This method works better than cooking it closer on a lower heat.

2. *Preheat the broiler.* I allow about 20 minutes for the broiler to heat to maximum.

3. *Leave the oven door open while broiling.* If you shut it, you

are baking as well as broiling. Besides, I like to see and smell and hear my fish broiling.

4. *Get thin fillets close to the heat.* The sliding racks in most electric ovens are adjustable. For small fillets, put the rack in the topmost position, then put your broiling pan on it. For thin fillets, you may have to put some sort of spacer under the broiling pan in order to get the fish closer to the heat. Two inches isn't too close for thin fillets. A disgruntled female once told me that broiling too close to the heating element makes a mess in the oven, causing the grease drippings and basting liquid to pop and spatter. I don't deny it.

5. *Baste.* Most trout should be basted, usually with butter, a time or two while broiling. Often a leftover marinade is used for basting. Some people, however, object to using leftover marinade toward the end of the cooking period because it contains uncooked fish juices and blood. Think about it. In any case, an oily baste keeps the surface of the fish from drying out, adds flavor, and helps browning. How often you baste depends on the recipe, but thin fillets usually need only one treatment about halfway through cooking.

6. *Watch your business.* If you have to scrape your toast every morning, remember that broiling fish is a full-time job. This is especially true of thin fillets very close to the heat. A minute too long can ruin your trout.

Broiled Trout Fillets

I like this recipe with nice-size fish of 2 or 3 pounds. These should yield fillets about 1 inch thick. Note that I cook the dish with the aid of a heated cast-iron griddle. A hand-held round griddle can be used, but when cooking several fish, I sometimes use a rectangular griddle fitted across two stove burners.

> trout fillets
> butter
> onion slices
> salt and pepper

Preheat the oven broiler at 500 degrees. Heat the griddle on top of the stove, then melt a little butter on it. Place the fillets skin side down on the hot griddle, fit in some onion slices, and cook for 2 or 3 minutes without turning. Sprinkle the fillets with salt and pepper, then use a spatula to place the onion slices atop the fillets. (Do not turn the onion slices.) Brush a little melted butter atop the fillets and onion slices. Quickly place the griddle under the red-hot broiler, about 3 inches from the heat. Broil for about 5 minutes.

Broiled Soy Trout

Soy sauce lends a nice flavor to trout, but some marinades overdo a good thing. Broiled trout fillets merely basted with a suitable sauce are just right.

> 2 pounds boneless trout fillets
> ¼ cup butter
> 2 tablespoons light soy sauce
> juice of 1 lemon
> freshly ground black pepper to taste

Melt the butter in a saucepan, then add the soy sauce, lemon juice, and black pepper. Preheat the broiler. Coat the trout fillets with the sauce, then place them about 4 inches from the heat. Broil until done, about 10 minutes, basting twice. When done, the fish will flake easily when tested with a fork.

Variation: Whole trout can also be cooked by this method. With larger fish, you'll have to lower the broiling rack so that the outside of the fish won't burn before the inside gets done; the larger the fish, the lower the rack.

A. D.'s Favorite Broiled Trout

This is my favorite recipe for broiling small trout of about 10 inches. Larger trout can be filleted and cooked by the same method. Cook the fish for about 10 minutes per inch of thickness.

Adjust the rack so that the fish is about 4 inches from the source of heat. Note that large fish can't be cooked by this method; the outside will burn before the inside gets done. With large fish, lower the rack and increase the cooking time.

small trout, dressed whole
½ cup butter
juice of 1 large lemon
1 tablespoon Worcestershire sauce
salt

Preheat the broiler on high heat. In a small saucepan, melt the butter, and mix in the lemon juice and Worcestershire sauce. Baste the fish lightly on both sides, then arrange them on the broiler rack or in a hinged basket. Slide them under the heat and broil for 6 minutes. Carefully turn the fish with the aid of a thin spatula. Baste lightly, and broil for another 10 minutes, or until the fish flakes easily when tested with a fork. Carefully remove the fish, then place them directly onto serving plates or small platters. After basting again, sprinkle with salt to taste.

Broiled Trout Paprika

Here's a dish that I like to cook when I'm in a hurry. It's best to use boneless fillets from small trout so that the meat is no more than ½ inch thick. I use a cast-iron griddle to cook the recipe under my stove broiler. If you have a set of those neat oval fajita griddles (one griddle for each serving), by all means use them.

2 pounds boneless trout fillets
¼ pound butter
1 teaspoon paprika
salt

Preheat the broiler. Heat your griddle on a stove burner. Melt the butter and stir in the paprika, along with a little salt. Grease the griddle, quickly arrange the trout fillets on it, skin side down, and place under the broiler, 2 or 3 inches from the heat. Broil, basting once, for 5 or 6 minutes, or until the fish flakes easily when tested with a fork. Serve hot.

Broiled Lake Trout Wheels

Skin and fillet the trout, cut each fillet crosswise into 1-inch strips, and sprinkle on a little crushed dill, salt, and pepper. Roll each strip into a wheel, then pin with a round toothpick. Preheat the broiler. Make a basting sauce by melting ¼ cup butter and stirring in ¼ cup dry white wine. Baste the trout wheels, put them on a greased rack, and broil them 4 inches from the heat for a total of 10 minutes, turning once and basting lightly several times. Do not overcook.

Brook Trout Bradford Angier

This dish requires watercress, which can sometimes be purchased in produce markets—and can usually be found free for the picking in local trout streams. It works best with small trout, broiled with the head on. I usually start cooking the dish by preparing the watercress butter, which is served with the broiled trout.

Watercress Butter
¼ cup butter
2 tablespoons chopped fresh watercress
1 teaspoon lemon juice
½ teaspoon salt
⅛ teaspoon freshly ground black pepper

Melt the butter in a skillet or saucepan. Add the salt, pepper, lemon juice, and watercress. Cook over low heat until the butter starts to turn tan, by which time, as Angier says in *Gourmet Cooking for Free*, "everything will blend in a harmony as meltingly unforgettable as that of a Tchaikovsky theme."

Serve the sauce over broiled trout, prepared as follows.

The Trout
4 to 6 small whole brook trout
melted butter
1 teaspoon salt
¼ teaspoon black pepper
⅛ teaspoon paprika

Preheat the broiler. Butter and warm a broiling pan. Mix the salt, pepper, and paprika. Rub the trout with this mixture, then brush with melted butter. Place the trout on the pan. Broil 4 inches from the heat for about 8 minutes, or until the meat flakes easily on both sides. (Angier instructs us not to turn the trout, but I usually do turn them after about 6 minutes. If you choose not to turn them, heat the broiling pan to hot instead of warm.) Serve hot with watercress butter.

Horseradish Trout

The root of horseradish adds an unusual piquant flavor to broiled trout. Commercially prepared horseradish sauces can be purchased at the market and smeared onto the fish, but I prefer to baste mine with a butter sauce during cooking. The recipe calls for fillets, but lake trout steaks or wheels (see Broiled Lake Trout Wheels) about 1 inch thick can also be used.

1 to 2 pounds of trout fillets
½ cup butter
1 tablespoon grated horseradish root
1 tablespoon grated onion
salt to taste

Melt the butter in a saucepan. Add the other ingredients, then simmer on very low heat for 20 minutes. Keep warm. After heating the broiling pan, put the fish in skin side down. Broil 3 or 4 inches from the heat for about 10 minutes, or until the fish flakes easily when tested with a fork. Baste twice with the warm horseradish mixture while cooking. If the fillets are on the thick side, lower the rack and cook for a longer time.

Trout à la Nantua

At one time, Nantua, France, was famous for its freshwater crawfish, and a dish cooked or served "à la Nantua" still means one garnished with a crawfish sauce, although some books have substituted shrimp without noting the switch. Since edible crawfish thrive in virtually all of North America's streams, lakes, ponds, and even roadside ditches, this method of serving trout is a good one for the angler to know. At streamside, you can finely chop some crawfish tails and sauté them in the pan drippings left from pan-frying the trout, maybe with a few sprigs of fresh watercress.

At home, you may want make a more elaborate sauce. The simple recipe below will do quite nicely with trout, and I advise you to stay out of French cookbooks. If you dip into one of these tomes, you'll no doubt find that the recipe for Nantua sauce will call for some béchamel sauce and compound butter, which in turn will call for a good many other ingredients.

> 1 to 2 pounds trout fillets or small whole trout
> 1 cup crawfish meat
> butter
> 3 tablespoons heavy cream
> ⅛ teaspoon cayenne
> salt

After bringing 1 gallon or more of water to boil in a large saucepan, add a little salt. Drop live crawfish into the pot, and cook them from 3 to 5 minutes, depending on their size. Peel the crawfish tails. You'll need a full cup of cooked tail meat, which will require quite a few crawfish. It's best to catch a hundred or more, then eat what you don't need for the recipe. When peeling the crawfish, also be sure to get some of the "butter" out of the head section; to accomplish this, twist the tail back and forth a couple of times before pulling it loose from the head. The fat will be visible. Scoop out some of the head fat with a baby spoon, and mix it with the tails. Mince the tails, or mash them in a mortar and pestle; I use a chef's knife, first mincing and then mashing with the side of the blade. Melt ¼ cup butter in a saucepan. Add the crawfish tails, cooking and stirring for about 10 minutes. Stir in the cream and cayenne, then remove from heat. Keep warm.

Broil the fillets or whole trout, basting once or twice with a little butter and sprinkling on a little salt if wanted. Do not overcook. Top each serving of trout with warm Nantua sauce.

Garlic Trout

In America, butter seems to be a favorite fat for basting and sautéing trout. It's hard to beat for flavor, but some cooks quit using it years ago. I've never given up butter entirely, especially for sautéing, because I like the flavor of it—especially salted home-churned butter. But I do find myself using more and more olive oil. It makes an excellent baste and can be used in marinades. It also takes on the flavor of garlic nicely, and I am especially fond of using garlic oil for basting broiled fish.

To make garlic oil, I fill a jar with peeled garlic and simply pour the oil over it. The oil will be ready to use in a month or so. Often I'll use a little of the garlic oil and top the bottle again with fresh olive oil. I know of a dozen or so stands of garlic that grow wild, producing cloves as big as my thumb, and I like to gather these, dry them in the sun for a few days, and make up several quarts of oil. The oil preserves the garlic, which can also be used as needed. I also like to use wild onions in the same manner. These days I see more and more flavored olive oils on the market, and these can also be used to baste fish on the grill or in the broiler.

Broiled trout basted with garlic oil and sprinkled with a little salt is one of my favorite recipes. The oil can also be used as a baste for grilled trout, and in salad dressings, if you like garlic.

Mormon Trout

In response to an article that I wrote, a dentist from Minnesota took me to task for poking a little fun at George Leonard Herter, author of *Bull Cook and Authentic Historical Recipes and Practices* and party to the old Herter's mail-order outfit. The dentist said I should show my teeth and genuflect to the north whenever I mention the man's name. Maybe. But I'll have to laugh a little, too, at some of Herter's more outrageous statements. In this recipe, for example, he says that the bullhead is a char and a close relative to brook trout. (What would L. L. Bean say about that?) In any case, Herter says that during their first winter in Salt Lake valley, the Mormons ate wild sego lily, dandelion roots and leaves, mule deer, prairie dogs, oxen, and trout. The trout, Herter says, were cooked as follows.

> trout, dressed whole
> 2 tablespoons melted butter
> water
> crushed sage leaves
> salt and pepper

Preheat the broiler at 450 degrees. Select a shallow broiling pan with enough rim to hold a little water. Pour ¼ inch of water into the pan, and pour 2 level tablespoons of melted butter on top. Place the dressed trout into the pan, then sprinkle them with crushed sage leaves, salt, and pepper. Adjust the rack so that the fish will be 5 inches from the heat. Broil the fish for 6 minutes. Turn carefully, then broil for another 6 minutes. Larger trout will require longer broiling times; test the fish with a fork for doneness. Serve with bread and butter.

Note: The sage leaves used in the recipe above may be from the sagebrush (genus *Artemisia*), which grows on the plains and is kin to the European tarragon, the leaves of which are also placed on fish before cooking. Sagebrush is different from the sage of Mediterranean origin (genus *Salvia*) that is commonly sold in spice markets. The American Indians chewed the leaves of sagebrush to help relieve stomach gas and used it to make an aromatic hair tonic. The plant was also used in various American folk medicines. Genus *Salvia* was used in European medicines long before its culinary properties were appreciated, and, according to Euell Gibbons, sage was originally added to sausages and stuffings to counteract indigestion and flatulence. An old wives' tale has it that sage mixed in tea would restore color to gray hair—and that teeth will be whiter if they are rubbed with sage leaves. I just thought that maybe our Minnesota dentist might like to have that information, along with Herter's Mormon Trout recipe.

SIX

Steamed and Poached Trout

Although I am guilty of sometimes vigorously boiling fish heads and bony parts for making soup and fish stock, the low-heat simmer is the real secret of good poached fish. And you don't want to cook them too long, either. Ideally, the poached fish should be moist and firm, not mushy. It's very easy, if you have the right equipment. The French, who are master poachers, have long pans designed for holding large fish with a minimum amount of water or poaching liquid. The pan, which sits across two stove burners, usually has a lid, as well as a rack that keeps the fish from direct contact with the bottom and helps in removing it intact. If you don't have such a pan, you might consider buying one, especially if you catch plenty of large fish and like them poached. I don't own such a poaching pan; I usually make do with an oblong fish fryer. For smaller fish and fillets, however, a long pan isn't necessary.

Poaching the fish in a Court Bouillon (chapter 13) enhances the flavor. If you don't want to make a production out of all this, just add a chopped rib of celery and celery tops to some salted water. I also like to add a bay leaf or two.

Steaming fish is also very easy if you have the right equipment. A fish-poaching pan can be used simply by elevating the rack and using only a small amount of liquid in the bottom. A Chinese bamboo steamer is very good for steaming small to medium-size fish, fillets, or steaks.

Poaching or steaming can also be used to precook fish for

recipes that call for fish flakes (see chapter 7). Poached fish is usually much better than leftover fish for these recipes.

Easy Poached Trout

If you don't have time to prepare Court Bouillon or a fancy poaching liquid, here's a good recipe to try. You can purchase canned clam juice at the supermarket or use the juice from fresh clams or oysters. The juice from oysters that are on the salty side is especially good for poaching, I think. Strain the juice from fresh clams or oysters before using.

> 1½ pounds trout fillets, skinless
> 1 cup clam or oyster juice
> 2 tablespoons butter
> 1 medium onion, minced
> 1 teaspoon minced fresh parsley
> salt and pepper

Heat the butter in a large skillet. Quickly cook the fillets for 1 minute on each side; remove to drain. Add the onion to what's left of the butter, then sauté for 5 minutes. Stir in the parsley, salt, pepper, and clam or oyster juice. Bring to a boil, add the trout fillets, reduce heat, and cover. Simmer for 5 to 6 minutes, or longer if your fillets are very thick. When done, the fish will flake easily when tested with a fork. Serve hot with hot buttered French or Italian bread. I also like to sprinkle some freshly ground black pepper over the fillets.

Trout Peru

According to *McClane's New Standard Fishing Encyclopedia and International Angling Guide,* the world's highest trout fishing is at Lake Titicaca in Peru and Bolivia—15,000 feet above sea level. Although insect life is sparse at this altitude, rainbows stocked in the lake grew fast, and during the 1950s Titicaca was noted for its large trout. The key to the fishery is a baitfish called *pejerrey,* which can be matched, McClane says, with a long silver-bodied streamer.

Peru has a wonderful cuisine, as this poached trout will show. The recipe calls for sour oranges. These are similar to the Seville oranges and the sour "wild" oranges of Florida, which are used in some Cracker kitchens to great advantage. For the 2 sour oranges, you can substitute 1 regular orange and 2 lemons or limes. Also, you can use only 1 or 2 colors of bell peppers, if you prefer.

> 3 pounds pan-dressed trout
> sea salt, crushed
> ½ red bell pepper, chopped
> ½ yellow bell pepper, chopped
> ½ green bell pepper, chopped
> 2 cloves garlic, minced
> juice of 2 sour oranges

Pat the pieces of trout dry, coat on all sides with crushed sea salt, and set aside for 1 to 2 hours. Bring 1 cup of water to boil in a large pan (with a tight-fitting lid) or electric skillet, then add the garlic, peppers, and orange juice. Boil for a few minutes. Rinse the salt off the trout pieces, and lay them into the pan on top of the peppers. Cover tightly, reduce heat, and simmer for 10 to 15 minutes, or until the fish flakes easily when tested with a fork. Spoon some of the pan liquid over each piece of fish, and serve at once.

Russian Trout

Cooking with ground walnuts and walnut sauces is popular in the Caucasus area, especially in the Republic of Georgia, and has now become a part of Russian cuisine. I would have called this recipe Georgian Trout, but that term is too easily confused with the state of Georgia. In any case, Georgia has several good streams (some flowing from ice-capped mountains westward into the Black Sea, and some eastward into the Caspian) that were, at least at one time, full of good trout as well as roe-bearing sturgeon. The Russians are fond of trout, and those from Lake Sevan in Armenia, due south of Georgia, are considered to be delicacies. One species of trout, called *ishkhan,* or "prince," has silver scales and red-rose meat. For this recipe, brook trout 8 to 10 inches long are just as good. Since this dish is served cold, it is great for a hot summer day.

Walnut Sauce
1 heaping cup walnut meats
¼ cup Fish Stock (chapter 13)
1 small onion, grated (golf ball size)
4 cloves garlic
¼ cup white wine vinegar
1 tablespoon chopped fresh mint leaves
salt and white pepper

Grind the walnuts in your mortar and pestle, or pound them, into a coarse meal. Add the garlic, salt, and pepper, crushing again until the garlic is pulverized. Mix in the grated onion, vinegar, and chopped mint. Slowly stir in some Fish Stock until you have a sauce. Chill until you are ready to eat.

The Fish
4 small trout
¼ cup white wine vinegar
salt

Dress the fish, and put them into a pan with just enough water to cover them. Add the wine vinegar and a little salt. Bring to a light boil, cover, reduce the heat, and simmer for 15 minutes. Carefully remove the fish, retaining the broth. Put the fish onto a suitable serving platter, and refrigerate until you are ready to serve.

The Garnish
6 green onions, with half of tops
fresh parsley

Using a chef's knife, mince the parsley and onions. Mix these together, then sprinkle over the fish. Pour the sauce over the garnish. I like some slices of bright red home-grown tomatoes on the side.

Chilled North Country Trout

I got this recipe from *Wilderness North,* by Dan Gapen, Sr., the son of the man who invented the muddler fly. It can be used to cook a small salmon as well as a trout.

The Fish
1 whole trout, 2½ to 3 pounds
1 medium onion
1 large carrot
2 tablespoons chopped parsley
juice of 1 lemon
1 tablespoon salt
sliced tomatoes for garnish
sliced cucumbers for garnish

Clean the trout whole, then wrap it in cheesecloth; it helps to have enough cheesecloth sticking out at each end to serve as handles. Pour 1 quart water into a pan long enough to hold the fish straight without bending (a French poaching pan is ideal). Turn on the heat, then add the salt, onion, carrot, parsley, and lemon juice. Heat the water to a rapid boil, reduce heat, and simmer for at least 10 minutes. Turn up the heat, lower the fish into the pan, bring to a new boil, reduce the heat, and simmer for 25 to 30 minutes, depending on the size of the fish. It's best to turn the fish once during cooking. Remove the pan from the heat, cool somewhat, and then place it into the refrigerator to chill. When you are ready to serve, remove the fish from the liquid, and peel off the cheesecloth and skin. Pour the Sour Cream Dressing over the fish, then garnish with sliced tomatoes and cucumbers.

Sour Cream Dressing
1 cup sour cream
2 tablespoons prepared horseradish
3 tablespoons chopped stuffed olives
½ teaspoon salt

Mix all the ingredients, then chill for at least 30 minutes. Serve over the chilled fish.

Poached Trout with Mustard Sauce

I like to cook this dish with a 2- or 3-pound fish, poached whole. It's best to use a Court Bouillon, but salted water can be substituted.

The Fish
whole trout
Court Bouillon (chapter 13) or water
salt
garnish

Put the fish onto a piece of cheesecloth and wrap it. Twist the ends and tie them off to form handles. Place the fish into a suitable container, and completely cover with Court Bouillon or water. Then remove the fish, and bring the liquid to a hard boil. Lower the fish carefully into the container, and poach—do not boil—for about 30 minutes, or 10 minutes per inch of thickness. Remove the fish, saving the liquid for the sauce, and place it onto a heated serving platter. Carefully remove the skin. Line the sides with lemon wedges and freshly washed parsley or other colorful garnish.

Mustard Sauce
2 cups Fish Broth (chapter 13)
½ cup dry white wine
½ cup half and half or light cream
3 tablespoons butter
2 tablespoons flour
2 tablespoons prepared mustard
salt and pepper

Melt the butter in a skillet or saucepan, and stir in the flour with a wooden spoon. Gradually pour in the Fish Broth, stirring as you go. Add the wine, salt, and pepper. Simmer for 5 minutes or so, then remove the pan from the heat. Stir in the mustard, then stir in the cream. Put the sauce into a suitable container, then serve it with the fish. The sauce also goes nicely over boiled new potatoes, which can be served with the fish.

Steamed Trout with Tofu

Here's a steamed dish that I like to cook. It works best with boneless fillets from trout of 12 or 13 inches. You can also use whole trout for the recipe if you increase the cooking time.

> 1 pound boneless trout fillets
> 1 cake (10-ounces) tofu
> 6 green onions, with half of tops
> 2 cloves garlic, minced
> 1 tablespoon sake or vermouth
> 1 tablespoon soy sauce
> 1 tablespoon peanut oil
> 1 teaspoon sesame oil
> ¼ teaspoon sugar
> ¼ teaspoon grated fresh ginger root
> black pepper

Although the Chinese like to slice their green onions lengthwise and put them on at the last moment, I prefer to slice them crosswise and sauté them in a skillet for a few minutes in peanut oil, along with the minced garlic. Add the sake, soy sauce, sesame oil, ginger, sugar, and pepper to the skillet, and keep warm while you rig for steaming. Slice the tofu into ½-inch slices, then arrange them on a plate or platter that fits into the steamer. Arrange the fillets, skin side down, atop the tofu, then spread the sauce evenly over the fillets. Steam for 20 minutes. Serve hot with plenty of rice and vegetables.

Vietnamese Steamed Trout

The Vietnamese are fond of seafood, and they often cook with fish sauce, called *nuoc mam,* which is similar to the old garnum of Imperial Rome. It can be found in ethnic markets and some supermarkets. The recipe below also calls for dried mushrooms, which can be found in the oriental section of some super- markets. Use the Chinese black mushrooms if available; if not, try the dried shiitake. You can also dry your own wild mush- rooms. The Vietnamese use lots of fresh cilantro (also known as fresh coriander or Chinese parsley) in their cuisine, and the flavorful root of this plant is sometimes used along with the tops.

Be sure to try this recipe on freshly caught trout. Use small trout whole, or use fillets of larger fish. You can also pan-dress the fish to make them fit your steamer.

    2 trout, about 10 inches long
    1 cup thinly sliced fatty pork
    6 dried black mushrooms
    4 tablespoons fish sauce
    4 shallots, thinly sliced
    1 tablespoon chopped cilantro
    1 tablespoon grated fresh ginger root
    1 teaspoon sugar
    salt and pepper

If the fish are whole, make 3 diagonal cuts on each side. Place the fish onto a shallow platter or suitable container that will fit into the steamer. Rig for steaming. (See directions earlier in this chapter.) Mix the pork, shallots, ginger, sugar, fish sauce, salt, and pepper. Coat the fish with this mixture, and let stand for at least 30 minutes. Meanwhile, place the mushrooms in water and soak for at least 15 minutes; then drain them and cut into matchstick-size pieces. Place the mushrooms on top of the fish. Bring the steamer to heat, then place the fish inside. Steam for 30 minutes. Sprinkle on the cilantro, along with a little salt and black pepper. Steam for another 2 minutes. Serve hot with rice and vegetables. The Vietnamese eat lots of raw vegetables, so a large tossed salad would be a good choice. Often the Vietnamese end the meal with fresh fruit.

Note: The peoples of Indonesia, Thailand, and Vietnam eat lots of fish and shellfish. For more of their recipes, see a book called *Flavors of Southeast Asia,* from which the above recipe has been adapted.

Chilled Trout with Easy Pomegranate Sauce

Usually, trout that is to be served cold is first poached and then chilled in the refrigerator. It is often served with a cold sauce. Dill sauce is a favorite, but I also like a colorful pomegranate sauce. (Pomegranates are available in some markets in the fall.) I prefer small, whole trout, but fillets of larger fish can also be used. The trout can be poached in plain or salted water, but it's better to use a Court Bouillon or special poaching liquid.

> 4 small trout or fillets from larger fish
> Court Bouillon (chapter 13) or salted water
> juice from seeds of 1 pomegranate
> juice from 1 lemon
> ½ to 1 tablespoon honey, to taste
> 1 teaspoon cornstarch
> 1 tablespoon cold water
> fresh parsley for garnish
> lemon wedges for garnish
> pomegranate seeds for garnish

Mix the pomegranate juice, lemon juice, and honey. Heat to a bubble, then add a little cornstarch paste, made by mixing the cornstarch into 1 tablespoon cold water. Heat and stir constantly until the sauce thickens a little, then put it into a serving bowl and refrigerate. Poach the trout in salted water or Court Bouillon for 10 or 15 minutes, or until it flakes easily when tested with a fork. Do not overcook. Remove the skin from the poached trout, and chill the fish. Serve cold with pomegranate sauce. Garnish with lemon wedges, chopped fresh parsley, and pomegranate seeds. The garnish makes a pretty dish, as well as a tasty one.

SEVEN

Flaked and Leftover Trout

One of these days, I have predicted, flaked fish will be as popular as ground beef and will be sold both fresh and frozen in our supermarkets. I say this because there will be more and more demand for a fish diet, and fish flakes make an ideal way to serve fish to people who think they don't like it. As a rule, I prefer a white, low-fat, naturally flaky fish flesh for this purpose. Large-mouth bass, for example, is perfect if poached for a few minutes before flaking. So is codfish.

Trout can also be used for this purpose and makes a very good change of pace if you are tired of eating fish. Leftovers can be used, but freshly poached or steamed fish are better. Some of the recipes given here are quite traditional.

Trout Croquettes

This dish can be made with leftover trout, preferably poached. You can also poach or boil trout until it flakes easily when tested with a fork, then flake out 2 cups.

> 2 cups flaked trout
> 1 cup cream of mushroom soup
> 1 tablespoon light rum
> dry bread crumbs
> salt and pepper
> peanut oil

Mix the fish, cream of mushroom soup, rum, salt, and pepper. Chill in the refrigerator. Rig for deep frying, and heat the oil to 375 degrees. Shape the fish mixture into patties, roll in bread crumbs, and fry until browned.

Kedgeree

There must be a hundred recipes for this old dish. Adapting it from East Indian cookery, the people of the British Isles have used it for a long time, in one variation or another, for combining trout or salmon with rice. True to the East Indian connection, this particular version contains curry. (Leave it out if you don't like it.) The dish is best when made with moist steamed or poached fish, but it can be made with any good leftover trout.

> 2 cups flaked trout
> 1 cup long-grain rice
> 2 cups water
> 2 hard-boiled chicken eggs, chopped
> 1 large onion, chopped
> ¼ cup cream
> 1 tablespoon butter
> 1 tablespoon chopped fresh parsley
> 2 teaspoons curry powder (optional)
> salt to taste

To prepare the rice, bring 2 cups water to a boil, add the rice and a little salt, bring to a new boil, reduce the heat to low, cover tightly, and simmer for 20 minutes. Do not peek. Melt the butter in a small skillet, and sauté the onions for about 5 minutes, or until they are soft. If you are using leftover fish, mix all the ingredients in an ovenproof serving dish, and heat in the oven. If you poached your fish while the rice was cooking, mix everything while the fish, rice, and sautéed onions are hot.

New England Kedgeree

Here's an old New England variation on the classic kedgeree. The ingredients call for ½ cup "top milk." I assume that this is milk that is rich in cream, since cream rises to the top of unprocessed milk. If you've got your own cow, try top milk. If not, use half and half.

> 2 cups flaked cooked trout
> 2 cups cooked rice, steaming hot
> ½ cup half and half
> 4 hard-boiled chicken eggs, chopped
> 2 tablespoons minced fresh parsley
> salt and pepper

Mix all the ingredients gently, and place in the top unit of a double boiler, with a little water in the bottom unit. This will help heat the dish without burning the bottom. Serve when hot.

Trout and Cheese Casserole

This recipe—a great way to use leftover trout—calls for a batch of yogurt cheese. This is very easy to make if you have the filter basket from an old drip coffeemaker and some coffee filters. Simply spoon plain yogurt into the filter, and let the whey drip out overnight. The residue left in the basket is yogurt cheese.

> 2 cups trout flakes (cooked)
> cheese from 8 ounces yogurt
> 1 cup grated mozzarella cheese
> ½ cup grated Swiss cheese
> ½ cup grated cheddar cheese
> ½ cup dry white wine
> ¼ cup chopped fresh parsley
> 1 medium onion, grated
> salt and pepper

Preheat the oven to 350 degrees, and grease a shallow baking dish. In a bowl, mix yogurt cheese, Swiss cheese, cheddar cheese, white wine, parsley, grated onion, salt, and pepper. Carefully mix in the trout flakes. Spread the mixture evenly in a greased, shallow ovenproof dish. Top with mozzarella cheese. Bake for 30 minutes, or until the top starts to brown.

Trout Burgers

Here's a patty recipe that works with any kind of trout. Our boys like to eat the patties with lots of catsup on them; our daughter likes to squeeze lemon juice over them; I prefer them plain or with perhaps a small amount of Chinese oyster sauce. When preparing the fish flakes, it's best to steam or poach the fish until it flakes easily with a fork.

> 2 pounds trout flakes
> peanut oil
> dry bread crumbs or cracker crumbs
> 1 medium small onion, minced
> 1 tablespoon minced fresh parsley
> 2 large chicken eggs
> juice of 1 lemon
> Tabasco sauce
> salt

Lightly beat the chicken eggs, then mix in the lemon juice, parsley, onion, salt, and Tabasco. Carefully stir in the fish flakes, along with enough bread crumbs to hold the patties together. Heat ½ inch of peanut oil in a skillet, and brown each patty on both sides, turning carefully with the aid of 2 spatulas or a spatula and a fork.

Trout à la King

Here's a delicious dish that can be cooked with flaked leftover trout or, better, with flaked poached trout.

1 cup trout flakes
½ cup milk
⅓ cup chopped green bell pepper
⅓ cup chopped red bell pepper
⅓ cup chopped onion
1 tablespoon butter
½ tablespoon flour
salt and pepper
fresh parsley for garnish
stuffed olives for garnish

Sauté the bell peppers and onion in a little butter for about 5 minutes. Stir in the flour, and cook for 2 minutes. Stir in the milk and simmer—do not boil—for 15 minutes. Add the flaked trout, salt, and pepper, then simmer for 2 more minutes. Serve over toast halves, cut diagonally, and garnish with a sprig of fresh parsley and stuffed olives.

Trout Salad

Exact proportions aren't necessary for making this recipe, but as a rule I allow ½ pound fish (undressed weight) and 1 chicken egg for each person for a light lunch or as a side dish. Heavy eaters will require more.

1 trout, about 2 pounds undressed
4 hard-boiled chicken eggs
crisp lettuce
mayonnaise
olive oil and tarragon vinegar salad dressing

Poach the trout in salted water until tender. Skin the fish, then flake the flesh off the bones. Sprinkle the meat lightly with the salad dressing, tossing gently to coat all sides, and marinate in the refrigerator for 2 to 3 hours. Drain and serve on lettuce leaves, along with hard-boiled egg halves and mayonnaise.

Variation: Sliced vine-ripened tomatoes also go nicely in this salad.

Trout Loaf

Here's a basic recipe for a trout loaf, which can be made with leftover fish or from freshly poached and flaked fish (preferably the latter). Endless variations are possible, such as using Italian bread crumbs for a little more spicy flavor, or using different sauces.

> 3 cups flaked trout
> ¾ cup fine bread crumbs
> ⅓ cup butter
> 1 medium onion, minced
> 2 large chicken eggs, whisked
> 1 tablespoon chopped fresh parsley
> salt and pepper
> 1 to 2 cups warm Creole Sauce (chapter 13)

Preheat the oven to 375 degrees. Mix all the ingredients except the Creole Sauce. Grease a loaf pan of suitable size, then spread the mixture evenly in the pan. Bake in the center of the oven for 1 hour. Top the loaf with warm Creole Sauce. Serve hot.

Variation: Use cilantro instead of parsley, add ½ teaspoon chili powder, and top with salsa instead of Creole Sauce.

Dan Gapen's Lake Trout Patties

Dan Gapen is an author and tackle manufacturer who writes of the northern wilderness from the heart. Here is his recipe for cooking lake trout patties.

> 1 cup flaked trout
> 1 chicken egg
> ¼ cup cracker crumbs
> ½ teaspoon onion salt
> ½ teaspoon celery salt
> salt and pepper
> shortening or cooking oil

Mash the trout with a fork. Whisk the egg. Mix egg, trout, cracker crumbs, salts, and pepper. Shape into patties about ½ inch thick. Heat a little shortening in a heavy skillet or griddle. Cook the patties on both sides until they are a rich golden color. Serve hot.

EIGHT

Campfire and Streamside Trout

Some of the best camp or shore lunch trout are fried in a skillet. For a shore lunch, a large, deep skillet is desirable and can be taken along in a boat. For streamside cooking, a small, light skillet is in order simply because larger ones are too much to tote. If possible, I like to cook in cast-iron skillets, but the weight is often not practical. Instead of a skillet, consider using a small oval griddle, which is much lighter and does a super job of cooking a pair of small trout. Some griddles are flat without much lip, but some of the newer oval fajita griddles will hold a little oil or butter and are just right for sautéing a couple of small fish or fillets, for frying a couple of chicken eggs, and for whopping bears on the head. You can also eat out of these handy griddles.

Many of the recipes given in chapters 1 and 2 can be made in camp, and most of the grilling recipes in chapter 3 are suitable for cooking over coals. Other recipes throughout the book are especially suited for camp because they require few ingredients.

A number of camp stoves are available, and most of them do a good job. Some of the smaller ones won't get a large skillet or fryer hot enough to deep-fry fish, however, so it's best to test your gear at home before you have to depend on it in camp.

My first choice for cooking in camp is a hardwood fire. I enjoy the fire itself, and I like to cook on the coals. It's always best to build a large fire and pull a few coals aside for cooking purposes. A keyhole fire, built with rocks placed in the shape of a keyhole, is especially useful. The fire is built in the large end, and the cooking is done on the small end. The rocks on the small end should be close enough together and of a suitable height to hold the skillet or pot over the coals. A grate of some sort can also be used over the keyhole, either for grilling or for holding pots and pans. One of the most important things for cooking on a camp-fire is a pair of heavy gloves. These are especially useful for frying with large cast-iron skillets directly over hot coals, where the on-and-off method of heat control is used.

Some of the recipes in this chapter call for ingredients that can often be found along a stream or lake during fishing season.

Balsam Trout

Most of the books and articles on smoking and smoke-flavoring fish and meat warn us not to use any sort of resinous wood. Yet blackbirds smoked with myrtle are a delicacy on the island of Corsica. Although I still don't advise long cold-smoking with such woods, where tar might build up, I do recommend that you experiment with different flavors. Here's a cooking technique to try when you don't want to carry cooking equipment along on your fishing or camping trip in the Northeast, where the balsam fir grows. I found the recipe, by the way, in J. George Frederick's *Long Island Seafood Cook Book,* which attributed it to Belmont Lake Park and said that it can be cooked with any fish. Brook trout are hard to beat and are, I think, better suited for the tech-nique than low-fat fish, such as white perch.

>3 or 4 trout, 10 or 12 inches long
>salt and pepper
>green balsam twigs with leaves

Build a good fire, and let it burn down to coals. After dress-ing the trout, sprinkle them inside and out with salt and pepper. Gather a pile of balsam twigs. Separate the coals into two piles, and flatten one with a stick or tool. Quickly cover the coals with a bed of balsam twigs and place the fish on top. Add another layer of balsam twigs, and top with the other half of the coals. Let the fish cook for 30 minutes. Remove the top ashes and leaves carefully to keep the fish clean. Remember, however, that a few ashes won't hurt a thing.

Variation: You can use the same technique with fillets from larger fish. Cook with the skin side up, then you can peel off the skin before eating if the fish picks up too much ash.

Cherokee Mary's Carolina Trout

Anyone who makes a habit of encasing a trout or other panfish in clay before roasting it in the coals of a campfire ought to try this method. It calls for green corn shucks, but dry shucks can be used in a pinch, provided that they are soaked thoroughly in water. It is best to cook this dish when the young corn is just right for roasting, so that you can roast some corn right along with the fish.

First, soak some unshucked ears of young corn in salty water. Build a good wood or charcoal fire and let it burn down to hot coals. Dress the fish. Select an ear of corn for each fish, then place the rest of the ears onto the hot coals to roast, turning them every 5 minutes. Peel back the shucks and remove the ears from the rest of the corn, leaving the shucks attached at the base. Sprinkle each fish with salt and pepper, then stuff it with a pat of butter. Place each fish inside a set of shucks. Smooth the shucks down tightly, and tie with wet twine. Place the stuffed shucks onto the coals. Time it so that the fish are put into the coals about 20 minutes after the corn, which takes a little longer to cook. Then leave both corn and fish in the coals for 10 minutes, turning the fish once. Before ringing the dinner bell, remove both an ear of corn and a fish to test for doneness. If you prefer, you can serve the corn with the usual butter and salt.

Sumac Trout

I claim bragging rights to this recipe, which I devised to use whenever I find fresh sumac berries growing along a stream. That's right. Sumac. The berries are covered with hairs that are coated with malic acid, which has a pleasing tart flavor. Similar berries are used in the Middle East, and recipes from Apicus (the ancient Roman culinary sport) call for Syrian sumac. All of the American sumacs with red berries (genus *Rhus*) can be used. In fact, a pleasing drink, sometimes called Indian lemonade, can be made from the berries and a little sugar. Also, the early settlers used a sumac infusion as a substitute for lemon juice. Usually, the drink is made by sloshing some berries around in cold water. The berries don't have to be crushed, since most of the flavor is on the tiny hairs that grow on the surface. The liquid is then strained through a double thickness of cloth to get rid of the spent berries and the fine hairs that come off. (Note that washing the berries in the stream will rob them of flavor; also, a strong rain can wash the flavor off the berries, so it's best to get them during dry weather.) For the recipe below, make the sumac drink, then boil it until it is greatly reduced and tastes as strong as lemon juice.

> 1 or 2 small trout, less than 1 pound
> 2 or 3 tablespoons butter
> flour
> sumac concentrate
> watercress
> salt

Dress the trout with or without the head, depending on the relative size of your skillet, and sprinkle it inside and out with salt. Dust the trout lightly with flour. Rake a few coals away from the fire, then melt the butter in the skillet. Sauté the trout until done on both sides, turning once. Remove the trout to drain. Add the watercress and a little sumac concentrate to the skillet, stirring and shaking the pan for a few minutes. Taste and add more sumac if needed. Pour the sauce over the trout. Eat hot.

Note: Sumac berries grow in bunches and are very easy to gather. They can be stored in a dry place for winter use, or you can freeze the juice. Make a little extra strong juice by boiling as directed above, and try it in recipes that call for lemon juice. Then you can smile the next time you price a lemon in the supermarket. Note also that green or unripened grapes (sour grapes) can often be gathered along a stream or lake during fishing season. Juice from these (called *verjuice*) was a popular cooking ingredient during the Middle Ages and was used in Egypt, especially on fish. Sour grape juice is still used as a seasoning in the Caucasus, where it is called *abgora*. You can use it too in camp or at home. You may even like it better than lemon juice.

Beard's Blue Trout

Here's a good recipe for Blue Trout, or *Truite au bleu,* from James Beard.

"This famous dish is usually to be found only in restaurants specializing in Continental cuisine. However, since the fish must be live, we think that the bank of the stream in which they were caught is the perfect place to cook them. Have ready 1 quart of boiling water to which 1 cup of vinegar and 1 tablespoon of salt have been added. Keep the fish alive until cooking time, then clean quickly and plunge at once into the boiling liquid. Remove pan from hot part of the fire and allow to simmer for 8 or 9 minutes, or until the fish are *just* done. The skin will turn blue—hence the name. Serve with butter, lemon juice, and boiled potatoes, and do have a pepper mill or some whole pepper that you can crush for this classic dish of fish."

Note: The blue color is caused by the slime on the skin. If you scrub the fish, it won't blue properly.

Scottish Breakfast Trout

According to Frances MacIlquham's *Fish Cookery of North America,* this traditional Scottish breakfast recipe is sometimes called "wind-blown trout." A jackleg genealogist in the family has told me that the Livingston clan came to America from Scotland. I don't know about that, but I do know that both my father and grandfather loved lightly salted fish for breakfast. That's good enough for me.

Catch some small trout—no longer than 10 inches. Skin these, draw, and remove the gills, leaving the head on. Rub salt well into the body cavity and on the outside. The entire fish must be well coated with salt. Then run a fish stringer through both lips, and hang the trout in a cool place with good air circulation. Leave the fish hanging in the open air all night, or at least 10 hours.

When you are ready to cook, shake the trout in a bag with a little flour, and grill it over coals. Baste on both sides with plenty of melted butter.

Note: This breakfast dish can also be cooked on the patio grill or under a broiler in the kitchen. I put it in this chapter because a good breeze is often available when you are camping near a trout stream.

Campfire Togue

Called *togue* in parts of the Northeast, lake trout are best when they are drawn and cooked right away. This recipe allows you to cook a whole fish in camp without long utensils. The recipe is from *The Maine Way,* published by the Maine Department of Inland Fisheries and Wildlife.

"Start a good, hardwood fire, and let it burn down to hot coals. Clean one good-sized salmon or lake trout, or two average-sized fish. Put 2 slices of bacon and 5 slices of onion into the body cavity. Salt and pepper the outside of fish, then roll it up in a greased sheet of heavy paper followed by a dozen or more thicknesses of paper (newspaper is fine). Tie the package and soak in water for about 10 minutes. Dig a hole in center of fire, lay in wrapped fish, and cover with embers. Bake 25 minutes."

Planked Fish

The hardest part about this recipe is finding a suitable board; for this reason, the technique is seldom of much help in survival cooking. On the other hand, a campfire is very much in order.

You'll need a good hardwood board about 2 inches thick and a little wider than the fish fillet. Place the fish fillet skin side down on the board, then drive small nails around the edge of the fish to keep it from dropping off or sliding down. Fix the board at an angle of about 60 degrees to the ground. Wedging it between rocks or logs is usually sufficient, but be certain that it won't slip. It's best to make a trial setup before planking the fillet. The thicker the fillet, the farther it should be from the fire; the thinner, the closer. It's best to build a large fire, then rake some coals aside for cooking purposes. Then you can push away some coals or add more, as needed. A keyhole fire works nicely.

> large trout fillet
> fresh lemons
> melted butter
> salt and pepper

Build a good fire, then let it burn down to hot coals. Plank the fillet skin side down. Brush with a mixture of melted butter and lemon juice and sprinkle with salt and pepper. Angle the board over the fire, fish down. Cook until the fish flakes easily when tested with a fork. The exact cooking time depends on the thickness of the fish, the heat of the fire, and the distance of the fish from the fire.

NINE

Smoked Trout

Most trout are on the fatty side, and this makes them very good choices for both hot smoking and cold smoking. With hot smoking, the fish is subjected to smoke during the cooking process. There are several small commercial smokers on the market, and these do a good job if the manufacturer's instructions are followed. With cold smoking, the fish is not actually cooked. At one time, cold smoking was part of a lengthy method of preserving fish, and it followed a salt cure. There are several books about smoking fish and meats. There is even a recipe book for using smoked fish and meats. For openers, you may want to consider the following recipes and methods for both cold and hot smoking; these include notes on salt curing as appropriate.

Hot-Smoked Trout

This dish is only lightly cured before smoking and does not keep for a long time. Eat it hot or chill it before serving. Small trout, 9 inches or so, work best. Larger fish should be filleted or cut into steaks. The electric silo water smokers (without the water) are ideal for cooking this dish, but other rigs can be used. Try to hold the temperature down to 250 to 300 degrees.

>   trout
>   1 gallon water
>   ½ cup sea salt or table salt
>   ¼ cup brown sugar
>   1 tablespoon chopped parsley or celery tops

Mix the water, salt, sugar, and parsley. Put the fish into a nonmetallic container, and pour the brine solution over them. Marinate for 3 hours. Rig for smoking at a temperature of about 250 degrees. Smoke-cook until the fish flakes easily when tested with a fork.

Apple Wood Trout

This recipe works best for trout about 13 inches long. Cut the trout up the middle or down the back, so that they open flat. Do not skin or scale. The recipe calls for apple wood, but any good hardwood can be used if you don't tell anybody. Be sure to try crab apple if you have some handy. I prefer green wood over dry chips that have been soaked in water.

> several trout about 13 inches long
> 1 gallon water
> 1 cup salt
> 1 tablespoon brown sugar
> ½ teaspoon mixed pickling spices
> green apple wood

Clean the trout with or without heads, then cut down the middle so that they open flat. Mix the water, salt, sugar, and spices. Put the trout into a nonmetallic container, cover with the brine, and soak overnight. In the morning, rig for smoking. Rinse the trout in cold water, pat dry, and put them onto a rack (skin side down) in the smoker. Smoke at about 160 degrees, or until the fish is nicely browned and done; of course, the cooking time will depend on the type of smoker you are using and the conditions. This recipe will work in a silo-type water smoker, but I prefer to leave the water out of the drip pan. You can also use this recipe for smoking in a large covered grill, in which case the cooking time will probably be shorter, depending on the fire and other conditions. Do not overcook.

Russian Smoked Trout Salad

The Russians have several salads calling for caviar with either mayonnaise or sour cream. Here's one made with smoked trout, which I have adapted from Kira Petrovskaya's *Russian Cookbook*. Although it is billed as a salad, I make a whole meal of it.

½ pound boneless smoked trout, diced
4-ounce jar or tin of red or black caviar
3 medium potatoes, boiled and cubed
2 medium tomatoes, sliced
1 cucumber, sliced
½ head crisp lettuce
6 green onions, chopped with half tops
6 black olives, pitted
1 dill pickle, chopped
⅔ cup mayonnaise
1 tablespoon red wine vinegar
salt and pepper

Shred the lettuce, then mound it in a salad bowl, forming a crater in the center. Arrange the sliced tomatoes and cucumber along the sides of the mound. Gently mix the chopped smoked fish, potatoes, and dill pickle; put this mixture into the crater. Mix the mayonnaise, vinegar, and caviar, then spread over the salad. Mix the chopped onions and olives, along with a little salt and pepper, and scatter over the salad. Serve cold with bread. And vodka.

Hot-Smoked Salt Trout

Here's one of my favorite recipes for smoked trout. Before smoking, soak the fish in a brine for several hours, and then dry it in a breezy place (or under a fan) until a shiny pellicle forms. To make the brine soak use at least 2 cups salt per gallon of water. Fillet the fish, leaving the skin on, and put them into the salt brine immediately. If they are very fresh, do not wash the fish before brining; otherwise, rinse them in salted water.

The Fish
salted fillets from 6 medium trout
¼ cup melted butter

Build a charcoal fire in your grill or smoker unit. Let the coals burn until they are white all over. Then cover the coals with wet hickory chips or some other wet hardwood. I prefer green wood, and I often use pecan chips because they are readily available to me.

Grease the grill's rack, then place the fish on it, skin side down. Close the hood and let the fish smoke and cook for about 30 minutes. Then open the hood and baste the fish with melted butter. (I use a brush for this purpose.) Close the hood. Repeat the basting process every 10 minutes, adding more wood chips if needed, until the fish flakes easily when tested with a fork. This should take about 1½ hours of total cooking time, but a lot depends on your grill, on how hot your fire is, and on how close your grill is to the heat source.

While the fish is smoking, get a bowl and make the following sauce.

Hot Sauce
½ cup apple cider vinegar
½ cup honey
½ cup Creole or Dijon mustard
¼ cup Worcestershire sauce
1 tablespoon chopped parsley
2 teaspoons Tabasco sauce
about ⅛ teaspoon black pepper

Blend the ingredients, then bring to a boil. Reduce the heat and let the sauce cool down a bit, but keep it warm.

Serve the fillets on individual plates, skin side down, and spoon some hot sauce evenly over them. Have plenty of fillets for additional servings.

I like this dish with fresh grilled (roasted) corn on the cob. The salty folk who people the Outer Banks area of North Carolina are fond of eating watermelon with fish. Consider giving this a try—

the combination of hot smoked trout and cold watermelon is memorable.

Cold-Smoked Trout

At one time, salt-curing and cold-smoking trout served primarily as a means of preserving fish for later use. If the fish were hard cured—highly salted and dried—they would keep indefinitely. These days, now that we have mechanical refrigeration and deep freezers, the major use of smoke is as a flavoring agent, and the use of salt has been cut down drastically.

Before trying the recipe below successfully, you'll have to be able to smoke the fish in a relatively cool chamber. This is usually accomplished by having the actual fire some distance away from the smoke chamber and connecting it with stovepipes or some such arrangement. The heat can be generated by wood, charcoal, or electric heaters. Usually, it is easier to cold-smoke in cool weather. It would, for example, be difficult to cold-smoke at 80 degrees in 90-degree weather. In any case, cold smoking must be done below 100 degrees, and, preferably, at 80 degrees or lower.

The first step to cold-smoking fresh fish is to wash them in a brine and drain them. Then dredge the fish with salt and place them in a salt-lined box. Let them sit overnight (or longer, depending on the hardness of the cure), then rinse them and let them dry in an airy place until a pellicle forms on the flesh. This should take about 3 hours. After the pellicle forms, cold-smoke the fish for 8 hours or longer. The fish should take on a golden color, and the flesh should be firm but pliable. (Drying the fish with long smoking will make them too hard for easy cooking.) Remember that these fish are neither cooked nor preserved. Either cook them right away or refrigerate them for a few days. Or freeze them.

Any size trout can be smoked. The larger specimens should be filleted or steaked. Some people add spices and brown sugar to the salt cure, but this is not necessary. I like to baste my fish with bacon drippings a time or two during the smoking process.

Cold-smoking is not difficult, but getting exact results time after time requires some experience and the proper equipment. A walk-in smokehouse is best for large production.

TEN

Salted, Pickled, and Canned Trout

The art of preserving fish at home has almost died out now that we have refrigerators and deep freezers. I'm not a survivalist nut, but it does give me some pleasure to know that I could get by without mechanical refrigeration. Also, I recommend that anyone try these old methods from time to time for culinary purposes. Salt trout, for example, has a texture and a flavor all its own. Some of the recipes that follow, especially for pickled fish, are not intended for long storage, however, so be sure to read each one carefully.

In this chapter I also cover fish that is eaten raw, as in seviche or gravlac. A friend who was telling me one night about eating seviche in a Mexican restaurant, saying that the fish is really cooked by the lemon juice, got upset when I told him that the fish really wasn't cooked. I have heard similar statements made about gravlac. Well, it's not cooked, either. A chef may tell you that it is cooked and you may want to believe that it is cooked. But it really isn't. Cooking requires some heat. My edition of *The Random House Dictionary of the English Language*, a book that is correct 95 percent of the time, defines *cook* this way: "to prepare (food) by the action of heat, as by boiling, baking, roasting, etc."

Both seviche and gravlac are very good, though, if you aren't too squeamish about these matters. I prefer to make my own from fish that I have caught or otherwise know to be very fresh or to have been properly frozen.

Trout Seviche

This dish, perhaps of Polynesian origin, is quite popular in Latin America as an appetizer or first course. Some people prefer seviche with lean white-fleshed fish, such as red snapper. Others prefer a fatty fish, such as Spanish mackerel. Small trout are halfway in between, and will please everybody. Ingredients vary, but most of the recipes contain chopped tomato, onions, and peppers. Lime or lemon juice is essential. I love this dish—provided that I have caught and dressed the fish myself. If you can't process the fish within hours of catching, it's best to freeze it in water until needed. Actually, freezing at 0 degrees F. or lower for several weeks will destroy any harmful bacteria in the flesh.

This version of seviche calls for thin fillets of small trout. A larger fish can be used, but it's best to cut the fillets into thin strips.

> 1 pound fillets of small trout
> juice of 6 limes or lemons
> 2 fresh tomatoes, peeled and chopped
> 1 medium onion, chopped
> ½ green bell pepper, seeded and chopped
> ½ red bell pepper, seeded and chopped
> 2 jalapeño peppers, seeded and minced
> ¼ cup olive oil
> 1 tablespoon red wine vinegar
> ¼ cup chopped fresh parsley (optional)
> salt

Wash the fillets, then place them in a deep nonmetallic bowl. Cover them with lime juice, stirring to coat well, and marinate in the refrigerator for at least 6 hours. Mix all the other ingredients in a small bowl, then drain the juice off the fish. Then pour the sauce over the fillets, toss, and serve cold with crackers.

Note: Although seviche is usually served as an appetizer, I find it to be an excellent light lunch on a hot summer day, served with plenty of crackers or bread thins.

Rakørret

This Norwegian dish is usually made these days with cultivated rainbow trout. Traditionally, the trout are processed in a wooden container that will hold about 4 gallons, but I have found a Styrofoam ice chest to be satisfactory.

If you want to try Rakørret, catch some trout of about 1 pound each, and fillet them. Put a layer of coarse salt at least 2 inches deep in the bottom of the container. (You may want to use rock salt for this purpose because sea salt is so expensive these days.) Add a layer of trout, skin side up. Do not overlap the trout. Add a thin layer of salt, covering all the fish but not piling it on. Add another layer of trout, and so on, until you fill the box or run out of fish. Top off with salt.

This dish is usually made in the fall, when the weather is cool, and the Norwegians merely sit the box outside in the sun for 3 to 4 weeks. If you live in a hot climate, turn the air conditioner down to 70 degrees and sit the box in a picture window that catches the morning sun. Be warned that this stuff smells loudly, so keep the lid on tightly.

Serve the trout thinly sliced, without cooking, with thin bread and a little hot prepared mustard. If you have fixed a whole box of these trout, only to find that you don't like them or that they are too strong or too salty for your taste, soak them in milk overnight to soften and sweeten them. Then dust them with flour and fry them in butter. Or flake off the meat and use it to make salt codfish balls, using any good New England recipe. In Boston, according to my copy of *Old-Time New England Cookbook*, salt codfish balls, Boston brown bread, and Boston baked beans are traditionally served up for breakfast on Sunday morning.

Ida's Pickled Trout

I am fond of pickled raw fish, and trout is one of the best to use for this recipe. Although the salt and vinegar will dissolve small bones, I usually work with skinless fillets. These are cut crosswise into fingers. Note that this recipe requires at least 9 days. Two weeks would be better.

2 pounds skinless trout fillets, fingered
2 quarts water
onion, thinly sliced
lemon, thinly sliced
2 cups pickling salt
2 cups white vinegar
1½ cups sugar
5 whole cloves
4 bay leaves
6 whole allspice
2 teaspoons mustard seed
2 teaspoons peppercorns

Mix the water and pickling salt in a nonmetallic container. Add the fish, stirring about, and rig a piece of wood, a plate, or some such weight on top of the fish in order to keep the fish completely submerged. Put aside for 48 hours.

In a saucepan of suitable size, bring the vinegar to a boil. Add the sugar, bay leaves, cloves, allspice, mustard seed, and peppercorns. Cool.

Layer the fish, onion slices, and lemon slices in small sterilized jars. Cover with the pickling solution, and cap the jars. Keep the jars in the refrigerator for 1 week or longer before eating the fish. The fish will keep for a month or so in the refrigerator. I like these with crackers and beer.

Variations: If you have juniper berries on hand, use them instead of the allspice. Also, add a little fresh dill if you have it.

Antipasto

This Italian dish is usually served as part of an appetizer or hors d'oeuvre spread. I like it for lunch, served with an assortment of crackers and cheeses. If you want to be a stickler, you'll point out that antipasto means before food or before feeding.

The ingredients below are merely suggestions. I have also added such things as cauliflower and Jerusalem artichokes. Foragers will want to try fiddleheads, catbrier, cattail shoots, edible mushrooms, and so on. I consider the trout and the tomatoes to be essential, however.

Although I list pickled trout below, you can use salt fish or seviche made with one of the recipes in this chapter. If you prefer, you can cut the trout fillets into chunks and sauté them in garlic butter until done. Then chill and use in the recipe. You can also use canned trout. Unless I am using salt-cured trout, I usually add a can or two of anchovies to my antipasto.

> 2 pounds trout fillets, pickled
> 1 can anchovies (optional)
> 2 fresh tomatoes, peeled and chopped
> 2 medium onions, chopped
> 2 carrots, thinly sliced
> 12 olives, sliced
> 1 rib celery with tops, chopped
> 1 red bell pepper, chopped
> 1 green bell pepper, chopped
> 2 tablespoons capers
> 2 cloves garlic, minced
> 1 tablespoon chopped fresh parsley
> 1 teaspoon mixed pickling spices tied in cheesecloth
> 1 teaspoon salt
> ½ teaspoon pepper
> olive oil

Cut the pickled trout into 1-inch chunks. Heat about 2 tablespoons of olive oil in a skillet. Sauté the chopped onion for 5 minutes. Add the other ingredients, except for the trout, and simmer for 15 minutes, or until the carrots are soft. Discard the bag of spices. Cool and put into a nonmetallic bowl. Carefully stir in the trout chunks, cover, and refrigerate for 6 hours or longer. Serve chilled, along with an assortment of crackers, finger foods, and cheeses, and some good red wine.

Note: You may want to add some wine vinegar to the mixture before refrigerating.

Norwegian Salt Trout

The Norwegians and other Scandinavians are fond of salt fish and sour cream. Salt-cured herrings and other sea fish are often used, after having been freshened overnight by soaking them in several changes of fresh water. The salt fish are cut into chunks, mixed with sour cream and other ingredients, and chilled. Thus, the fish are not really cooked. You can salt-cure and use trout in the same way, but I prefer to salt the fish lightly overnight and then poach them for a few minutes before using.

> 1 pound lightly salted trout fillets
> ½ cup sour cream
> ¼ cup minced onion
> 1 tablespoon minced fresh parsley
> juice of 1 lemon
> ½ teaspoon sugar
> 1 teaspoon chopped dill

Salt the fillets overnight. Place the salted fillets into a shallow pan, cover with water, add the chopped dill, and bring to a boil. Reduce heat, and simmer for a few minutes, until the fish are cooked through. Do not overcook. Remove the fillets from the pan, and cool. Remove the skin, and cut the fish into 1-inch chunks. Mix the sour cream, onion, parsley, lemon juice, and sugar. Carefully mix in the trout chunks, and chill. Serve cold.

Canned Trout

Most modern authorities do not recommend canning fish or meat. The main concern is botulism, a deadly food poison caused by a bacteria that thrives in the absence of oxygen. If the canned food is processed properly, sealed properly, and stored properly, it is perfectly safe. Usually, a contaminated jar will be under internal pressure, causing the lid to bulge. I always check the lid, and I always cook canned fish (except for tins of sardines) before eating it; although cooking won't necessarily negate botulism, I feel better about it. Why I should feel squeamish about canned fish when I have eaten a thousand cans of salmon, tuna, and sardines, I don't know. In any case, you'll need a reliable pressure cooker and some jars with good seals. In the recipe below, I usually cut the trout into chunks, including the backbone and ribs. The canning process will dissolve the bones. The measures in the recipe below are for a pint jar filled with fish; measure each batch separately.

> trout cut into chunks
> ¼ cup vinegar
> ¼ cup tomato cocktail sauce
> 1 teaspoon salt
> 1 teaspoon brown sugar
> ¼ teaspoon pepper

Pack a sterilized 1-pint jar with chunks of trout until almost full. In a saucepan or bowl, mix the vinegar, sugar, salt, pepper, and cocktail sauce. Pour the mixture over the fish, seal the jar, and process in a pressure cooker at 10 pounds for 1½ hours. Although canned fish may be safe to eat right out of the jar, I always cook it again in another recipe. Most of the recipes for canned salmon, found in family cookbooks, will work just fine for canned trout. Also try canned trout in some of the flaked fish recipes.

Note: This is a good recipe for canning suckers and other bony fish.

Helen's Canned Fish Patties

My wife makes some good canned fish croquettes, but it is difficult to pin her down on what's in them. Oh, she knows the list of ingredients, but she is vague on the amounts, saying that she mixes it as she goes. After watching her in action, I have come up with the approximate measures.

1 pint jar canned trout
½ cup cracker crumbs
⅓ cup Bisquick
1 large chicken egg, whisked
salt and pepper
cooking oil

Mix the first 5 ingredients in a bowl, including the juice from the can of trout. Mix well, then shape into patties. Heat about ⅓ inch of cooking oil in a skillet. Fry the patties, turning once, until nicely browned on both sides.

Note: We had a patty left over from the last batch we cooked, and I ate it for lunch the next day in a sandwich. Spread plenty of mayonnaise on both pieces of bread, and top the cold trout patty with a thin slice of white Vidalia onion. Delicious.

ELEVEN

Soups, Stews, and Chowders

The world's great fish soups, stews, and chowders usually don't call for trout. More readily available and less expensive fish are generally used for this purpose, and, in fact, some of the fishermen's stews were developed with fish that were hard to sell on the open market, or with fish heads and bony parts from commercial fish. This doesn't mean that trout can't be used in these recipes to great advantage. Some very fatty lake trout, and maybe other very fatty individuals from other species, should be parboiled in separate water, then added to the soup.

Any good fish cookbook will contain a dozen or two recipes for fish soups, stews, and chowders. Here are a few of my favorites.

Trout Stew, Chilean Style

The people of Chile are fond of fish both from the sea and from the streams and inland lakes. Trout are not native to the area, but stock from Germany was established in 1905. In the streams live a freshwater crab, which trout love to eat. (So if you are planning to fly-fish the area, bring along your McCrabs.) Although the good ol' days have gone, very large fish were once taken in Chile, and, on down toward the Antarctic, large sea trout were taken from Tierra del Fuego.

The favorite food fish in Chile is a large congerlike species taken from the sea. For this stew, however, a trout will do just fine.

1 trout, 3 or 4 pounds
4 medium potatoes, thinly sliced
2 medium onions, thinly sliced
2 tomatoes, thinly sliced
⅓ cup rice
1 tablespoon olive oil
salt and pepper

Dress the trout and cut it into pieces—or fillet if you expect guests who may not know how to handle the bones. Pour the olive oil into a stove-top Dutch oven. Add a layer of onions and a layer of potatoes. Top this with the fish, then layer on the rest of the onions and potatoes. Sprinkle on the rice evenly, top with a layer of tomatoes, and season with salt and pepper. Cook over moderate heat for 5 minutes. Pour boiling water into the pot, slightly covering the ingredients. Cover tightly, then simmer slowly for 25 minutes. Add a little more water if necessary. Serve hot in soup bowls.

Variation: Quinoa, an ancient grain of the Andes, is still available in South America today and is also raised to a limited extent in the United States. I have never seen it in a supermarket, but it can sometimes be obtained from mail-order sources. Quinoa is sometimes used like rice in South American dishes and can be substituted in this recipe.

Legal Trout Chowder

I understand that it was at one time against the law in the state of Maine to put tomatoes into anything called *chowder*. Although the tomato is native to the New World, it was originally from Central or South America. The Spanish took it to Europe, but it was not well received and was even believed to be poisonous. It came to North America from Europe, but was not widely accepted as being fit to eat. In fact, it did not become widely accepted until World War II. So don't be too hard on those New Englanders who still won't allow it in chowder. Try this hardy old Colonial recipe, and you might even agree that the tomato isn't needed.

1 pound trout fillets, skinned
2 cups cubed potatoes
3 slices of bacon or a little diced salt pork
1 medium onion, diced
2 cups whole milk
2 cups water
3 tablespoons flour
salt and pepper

Cut the fish into 1-inch chunks. Fry the bacon or salt pork in a small skillet until crisp; drain the bacon, reserving the drippings. Put 2 cups water into a pot, and bring to a boil. Add the potatoes, cover, and cook for 5 minutes. Meanwhile, sauté the onion in the bacon drippings for about 5 minutes. Add the fish and crumbled bacon or salt pork to the potatoes, cover, and simmer for 5 minutes; at the same time, add the flour to the bacon drippings and onions, cook for a few minutes, then stir in the milk until well blended. Add the contents of the skillet to the chowder, and simmer for 5 minutes, stirring from time to time and adding a little salt if needed. Serve in bowls with hot bread. I like to grind some fresh pepper over my bowl of chowder, and I recommend that you have a pepper mill on hand for those who want it.

Trout Soup with Avgholemono Sauce

This is a Greek dish with many variations. Usually, the sauce is made with part of the soup.

The Soup
5 pounds whole trout
4 large onions, peeled and sliced
3 large potatoes, peeled and diced
2 ribs celery with part of green tops, chopped
2 tablespoons olive oil
salt and pepper to taste
2 quarts water

Fillet the trout, and cut the meat into bite-size chunks. Set aside. Put the head and bones of the fish into a pot, then cover with about 2 quarts of water. Boil for 1 hour or so. Strain the stock and discard the bones. (Or better, flake off the meat from the bones, add it to the soup later during the recipe, and discard the rest.) Reserve 1 cup of the stock for the sauce, then add enough water to the remainder to make 2 quarts. Add the potatoes, onions, celery, olive oil, salt, and pepper. Bring to a boil, cover, and cook for about 30 minutes. (While waiting, make the sauce recipe below and set aside.) Add the cubed fish to the pot, then simmer for 20 minutes. Stir in the Avgholemono Sauce. Serve hot.

Avgholemono Sauce
2 chicken eggs at room temperature
juice of 2 lemons
1 cup hot fish stock

Beat the eggs and add the lemon juice. Slowly stir in the cup of hot fish stock. Set aside until needed for the soup.

Trout Head Tea

Here's a recipe from Jamaica, which I have adapted from Helen Willinsky's book called *Jerk*. She says that the dish is usually served in a big mug or cup and that it is often made from parrot fish, which is half head and is very bony. Trout heads will do just fine, or you can use a combination of heads and backbones from fish that have been filleted.

2 pounds trout heads
2 quarts water
4 medium potatoes, cubed
1 fresh tomato, chopped
½ medium onion, diced
1 tablespoon chopped fresh thyme or ½ tablespoon
    dried thyme
1 whole Scotch bonnet pepper (or other hot pepper)
salt and black pepper

Bring the water to boil in a kettle of suitable size. Add the trout heads, cover, and simmer for 30 minutes. Remove the trout heads. Strain the stock, then return the liquid to the pot. Remove all the flesh from the trout heads, returning it to the pot. Throw out the bones. Add the other ingredients, then simmer for about 20 minutes, or until the potatoes are tender. Remove the pepper. Note that the Scotch bonnet pepper is left whole so that you get the flavor and not the heat. Break it at your peril. Serve the soup hot.

Helen Willinsky says that this soup is believed to have medicinal properties in Jamaica, much like chicken soup in some other parts of the world.

Kalasoppa

Here's a Finnish dish that goes nicely with rainbows or other trout. It's very easy to make and is especially tasty, I think, with new potatoes. If you don't have new potatoes, use 3 medium regular potatoes.

> 1 pound trout fillets, cut into small pieces
> 10 new potatoes, golf-ball size
> ½ medium onion, chopped
> 2 cups water
> 2 cups whole milk
> 1 tablespoon butter
> 1 teaspoon flour
> salt and pepper

Boil the new potatoes in 2 cups water for 10 minutes. Add the fish, onion, salt, and pepper. Simmer until the potatoes are done. In a bowl, mix the flour and milk into a paste; slowly stir the paste into the soup. Next, blend in the butter. Add a little more salt if needed. Simmer for another 2 or 3 minutes. Serve hot with plenty of bread. If you like freshly ground black pepper, take a few turns of your pepper mill over the soup.

TWELVE

Trout Roe and Surprises

I've already said that the trout angler has a culinary advantage over cooks who don't catch their own. Part of the reason is that the angler can have complete control of how his catch is handled en route from the water to the table. This in turn helps him select a wider range of recipes and offers a wider range of good eating. For example, most fish markets don't offer trout roe and liver. Both of these delicacies can be enjoyed by the angler—but they should be eaten when they are very fresh.

Some people will not want these parts, regardless of how fresh they are. Consequently, it might be best for the angler to cook these for himself unless he knows his guests quite well. There is something about liver that turns some people off, although they might eat it if you mash it up with a little mayonnaise and call it *pâté*. Anyone who likes chicken liver, however, is urged to try trout liver. In fact, most of the recipes for chicken liver can be used for trout liver. Because the trout liver is smaller, it usually requires less cooking time. When overcooked, it will become hard, dry, and strong. If I am frying or sautéing freshly caught trout, I'll often cook the liver right along with the fish.

The roe of trout is also very good, and most recipes for other kinds of roe will work just fine. Most of the time I cook the roe right along with the fish they came from, especially if I am frying the fish. Or you may prefer to sample the following recipes.

Scrambled Eggs and Trout Roe

Here's a very good way to use a small amount of trout roe, and I especially like this dish for breakfast. I don't include exact measurements for the recipe, but it's hard to go wrong if you are reasonable with everything. The ratio of roe to egg isn't critical, but it's best to use a little more of the egg by volume.

The instructions below are for small roe. If you have large, very mature roe, first poach the sacs in lightly salted water with a little lemon juice.

>   trout roe
>   chicken eggs
>   bacon
>   green onions
>   salt and pepper

Fry the bacon in a skillet. Remove the bacon to drain, and pour off most of the pan drippings. In a bowl, whisk the eggs. Break the roe sacs and squeeze the roe into the eggs, stirring as you go. Add salt and pepper. Chop a green onion or two (including about half of the green tops) and stir into the egg mixture. Heat the skillet and what's left of the bacon drippings. Scramble the egg mixture until done. Serve with bacon, toast, and sliced vine-ripened tomatoes. This is one of my favorite breakfast dishes, and I have been known to make it do for lunch as well.

Variations: If you have a lot of people to feed and not much roe, add some cooked flaked fish. Also try this dish with sliced salt pork instead of cured bacon.

Trout Roe on Toast

Here's a good way to serve trout roe to people who may be a little squeamish. I like it for a light lunch, or even a late breakfast, served with a strip or two of bacon and a cold, sliced vine-ripened tomato.

113

½ pound roe
salt water
juice of 1 lemon
¼ cup butter
1 medium onion, minced
2 tablespoons flour
½ cup cream
2 beaten chicken egg yolks
hot buttered toast

Poach the roe in salted water and lemon juice for 15 minutes. (Do not boil the roe.) Drain the roe, remove the membrane, and mash the roe in a bowl. Melt the butter in a skillet, then sauté the onion for 5 minutes. Slowly mix in the roe and flour with a wooden spoon. Cook for a few minutes, stirring constantly, until the mixture starts to brown. Stir in the cream. Then stir in the beaten egg yolks. The eggs should get very hot but should not boil. Remove from heat. Serve over toast with bacon.

Skillet Liver

I am fond of eating liver in camp, and venison liver sautéed in bacon drippings along with onions and mushrooms is a favorite. You can also use fresh fish liver, or perhaps liver from small game, such as squirrels or rabbits, or from game birds. The recipe below calls for trout livers, but if you don't have enough of these to feed everybody, add some chicken liver or rabbit liver.

trout livers
bacon
onions, sliced
fresh mushrooms, sliced
salt and pepper

Fry a little bacon in a skillet. Pour off most of the pan drippings, then sauté the fresh trout liver, sliced mushrooms, and sliced onions for a few minutes. Do not overcook. At the last minute, stir in some salt and some freshly ground black pepper. Add the strips of crisp bacon back to the dish and serve.

Variation: Stir in a little red wine during the last few minutes of cooking.

Broiled Livers for the General

I got this recipe from *A General's Diary of Treasured Recipes* by Brig. Gen. Frank Dorn, who said that he got it, with a few minor additions, from the Blue Bell Cafe in Saint Ignace on the Upper Peninsula of Michigan, where it was served during whitefish season. It can also be cooked to advantage with fresh trout livers, as follows.

> 8 to 10 trout livers
> ½ cup butter
> ½ pint dry white wine
> ½ cup brandy
> 2 tablespoons Worcestershire sauce
> ⅛ teaspoon Tabasco sauce
> 8 whole cloves
> 8 peppercorns
> 1 teaspoon caraway seeds
> 1 teaspoon ground ginger
> 4 bay leaves
> salt and pepper
> flour

Mix all the ingredients except the livers and the flour in a saucepan. Boil for 2 or 3 minutes. Pour the mixture over the livers in a suitable container, and refrigerate for at least 6 hours. Then remove the livers from the marinade sauce, drain, reserving the sauce, and arrange them in a broiling pan. Place the rack about 4 inches from the heat, and broil the livers for 5 or 6 minutes, turning once.

Strain the sauce into a saucepan. Bring to a slow boil, stirring in a little flour to thicken it. Pour the sauce over the livers, and serve at once. Garnish with white radishes, the general says.

An Ojibway Treat

In the May 1967 issue of *Field & Stream*, Ted Trueblood published a story about a fishing trip he made to Lake Nipigon, in Ontario, with Bill McDonald and several Ojibway Indians. He and Bill feasted for several days on fillets of what he called big coaster brook trout, usually fried or grilled. The Indians, however, preferred to put the heads into a kettle of salted water and boil them for about 10 minutes, then gnaw and pick out the meat.

Later, Trueblood says, he got to thinking about this and started experimenting with fish heads. He started wrapping the heads of large salmon or lake trout in foil and roasting them directly in the coals while grilling the remainder. Also, he says, you can wrap half a dozen heads of smaller trout in foil and cook them directly on top of the coals. Trueblood didn't give any details, but I have found that the heads from 1- to 2-pound fish should be cooked for about 30 minutes. Heads from 10-pounders will take 1 hour, and the package should be turned at least once. It also helps to sprinkle the heads with a little salt and add an onion or two or perhaps some wild onions or wild garlic.

Experiment with this in camp or even on your stove-top grill, and you'll stop throwing away the heads of trout and other good fish. If you don't want to cook them with the fish, freeze them in water for later use. They're too good to throw away. They might well be the best parts, as the Ojibway know, if you have the time for nibbling. Accomplished backwoods nibblers and international gourmets also know that the tongues are choice parts, and in Asia the eyeballs are considered delicacies. I'll leave that up to you.

Dressing the head for the pot requires no special treatment. Some people remove the gills, but I confess that I usually leave them in. I don't eat them, but I don't see that they hurt anything.

Bony Parts

In addition to the heads, the backbone and ribs of trout contain some good meat that is often thrown out after filleting. These bones can be used in soups or to make Fish Stock, as described in chapter 13. When frying filleted fish, I also like to fry the backbone, then eat the meat like corn off a cob. It fries up crisply and is very tasty.

Even the bones of fish have some food value and are a good source of calcium. The Indians of the Northwest used to pulverize salmon bones and use them in their soups and stews.

THIRTEEN

Sauces, Breads, and Go-withs

Some cookbook writers hold that the sauce is just as important as the fish, or that fish somehow isn't complete without sauce. The French are especially fanatical about sauces, and for that reason sole is their favorite fish because it is mild and takes on the flavors of even delicate sauces. The trout, by comparison, doesn't sauce too well—and really doesn't need saucing.

For this reason, I am not going into the various French sauces, such as allemande, normande, or velouté, that are essential to cooking specific recipes. Instead, most of the sauces listed here can be served on the side, take it or leave it. Tartar sauce, for example, is very good (although some writers consider it to be overworked) and can be used as a dip as well as a sauce. But I really prefer the taste of fish.

I'm including Court Bouillon and Fish Stock in this chapter. This smacks of French cookery, but don't worry; I'm not going very far in this direction. The Court Bouillon is used for poaching fish, and a basic recipe will do. Fish Stock is used in various recipes, or it can be thickened and used as a soup, somewhat like chicken broth.

This chapter also includes recipes for corn bread and hush puppies, and I'll start with some notes about American cornmeal.

Cornmeal: The Right Stuff. The meal that I highly recommend—stone-ground meal from whole-kernel corn—is not widely available in supermarkets. This kind of meal almost died out in America because the method of making it doesn't lend itself to large milling operations and wholesale grocery distribution. At one time, every town had several gristmills on nearby creeks, and these provided good fishing holes as well as breadstuff. Gradually the product dropped out of the market, except for pockets in parts of the South and in Rhode Island, and perhaps other places. This kind of meal seems to be making a comeback, thank goodness, along with other whole-grain meals and flours.

Cornmeal is an important ingredient in some fish cookery, but not in all. It is used to make hush puppies, essential for a real fish fry in some circles, and as a dusting or coating for the fish. The cornmeal that I recommend is ground from whole-kernel corn. It is stone-ground, a process that doesn't generate much heat. It should be used fresh, which means that it has a relatively short shelf life. In my part of the country, several local millers supply supermarkets with this meal and rotate the stock as necessary, just as bakeries rotate bread stock. Most of the large milling companies, however, offer a rather gritty cornmeal that is not made from whole kernels and is not stone-ground. The only advantage to this cornmeal is that it is easy to manufacture and has a long shelf life. I have said in another context that it is unfit for human consumption, and that even hound dogs won't eat it after they have tasted hush puppies made from the real stuff. I was joking, of course, merely stretching the truth a bit.

It's best to buy this kind of cornmeal from a store or outlet that keeps it fresh. It is available in extrafine, fine, medium, and coarse grinds. I recommend the fine grind for hush puppies and other fried breads. The fine grind can also be used to dust fish for frying, but I sometimes use extrafine. The extrafine, however, doesn't work for frying breads in hot oil, and it will sometimes pop open, leaving a fried shell. If you can't locate the meal, you can order it from Adam's Mill, Route 1, Midland City, AL 36350, telephone 205-983-3539. Buy a couple of 5-pound bags, and store the meal in the freezer.

Or buy a kitchen mill, a device that is becoming more common these days for making whole-grain flours without additives. Any good corn can be used, but some mills use special corns, often raised for them locally, that tend to be on the soft side. I may be wrong on this count, but I think that soft corn is easier to grind and makes better (less gritty) meal. The color of the corn doesn't make much difference, as long as it is white. Seriously, though, the color isn't as important as the grinding process. In the Southwest, even purple or blue cornmeal is used.

Before moving on, I must point out that most of the corn bread and hush puppy recipes in other books are designed for the processed cornmeals from the large milling companies. Bread made from these meals tends to be dry and gritty. In fact, I have a book on corn cookery in which the author says that corn bread is dry. Not mine. In any case, Livingston's rule states that the better the cornmeal, the less stuff you'll have to put into it in order to make succulent corn bread—which leads me to the next recipe.

A. D.'s Skillet-Fried Corn Bread

I confess that I never measure out the ingredients for my skillet-fried corn bread. Yet, it comes out exactly the same time after time. Oddly, it *wouldn't* come out the same if I measured everything precisely and refused to adjust. Cornmeal, like wheat flour, varies slightly from batch to batch, and maybe with the weather and the phase of the moon.

I start by mixing white cornmeal with hot water and a little peanut oil (or bacon drippings) until I have a mush that will drop nicely from a large spoon, making a piece about the size of a chicken egg. After stirring in a little salt, I let the mixture sit while I heat ⅝ inch of peanut oil in the skillet. Then I stir the batter again, and more often than not, add a little more water, as the batter tends to stiffen as it sits.

Next I spoon a little batter into the hot peanut oil. If the mixture is just right, the spoonful will flatten slightly as it settles on the bottom of the skillet. (A cast-iron skillet, of course, is required.) Proceed until the pan is almost full of bread. Cook on both sides over medium heat, turning once. When done, the outside of the bread should be golden and crunchy, but the inside should be mushy when hot. When the pieces are done to your liking, take them up with a spatula or tongs and let them drain on a brown bag. As they cool off a little, the inside will firm up considerably.

Although I don't measure the ingredients, I realize that most readers need some guidelines. The following mix will be about right for making enough corn bread to feed 4 people.

> 2 cups fine white stone-ground cornmeal
> 1 tablespoon peanut oil or bacon drippings
> 1⅞ cups hot water
> salt

Remember that the mixture will vary slightly from one batch to another, partly because there is a difference in cornmeals. It's best to start with the measures given, then add meal to thicken or water to thin until the mixture comes out of the spoon just right and flattens slightly as it slides into the skillet. Before starting, pour some hot water into a small bowl or cup, and dip the spoon into it from time to time to keep the batter from sticking.

Note: I confess that the recipe above and the one below have been lifted from my book *Bass Cookbook,* and variations have been used in my other books. On one level, this troubles my conscience, because it seems somehow wrong to sell the same recipe more than once. On a deeper level, however, I feel obligated to tell the readers of this book the plain truth: If impeccably made with the right stuff, my recipe is the best ever devised for cooking corn bread. I see no need to add beer and chicken eggs to it merely for the sake of variation. That sort of thing happens far too often in books and magazines, and is one reason why our recipes get longer and longer year by year.

Deep-Fried Hush Puppies

I think the original hush puppies were oblong in shape and about thumb size. They were made with a simple mixture of stone-ground cornmeal, water, and salt, similar to my corn bread recipe above, except that the batter is a little thicker so that the pieces hold their shape. That is still my favorite recipe for hush puppies, but some people will insist on adding all manner of stuff, from beer to chicken eggs. Most of these recipes are good, if they are properly made with the right kind of cornmeal. If you don't care for my simple mix, use your own recipe—or try this one.

> 1 cup fine stone-ground cornmeal
> 2 tablespoons all-purpose flour
> 1 large chicken egg
> ¾ cup buttermilk
> ¼ cup minced onion
> ¼ teaspoon salt
> ¼ teaspoon baking soda
> ⅛ teaspoon black pepper
> water if needed
> oil for deep frying

Mix cornmeal, flour, baking soda, salt, and pepper in a large bowl. In a small bowl, whisk the chicken egg, then stir in the buttermilk and onion. Slowly mix the liquid into the dry ingredients. Add a little water if needed to make a soft dough. Ideally, a small, round ball of the dough should almost hold its shape, but flatten slightly on a hard surface. Rig for deep frying at 350 degrees (not as hot as for deep-frying fish). Drop the hush puppies by the teaspoonful into the hot oil. It's best to scoop up the dough with a teaspoon and help shape it with your left hand, then drop it gently into the hot oil. If the hush puppy doesn't come off the spoon cleanly, dip your spoon from time to time in a cup of water. Fry until golden brown.

Variations: There are countless variations on this recipe, such as using beer instead of buttermilk. I like to mince a jalapeño pepper and add it to the batter, or maybe use a little Tabasco sauce. You can also use garlic instead of the onion.

Good Ol' Boy Hush Puppies

Use any good recipe for hush puppies, but cut the water measure in half and make up the difference with beer. Usually, these are cooked on the patio with a gas-heated fish cooker. It's best to cook these for a group so that you'll get various opinions on what kind of beer is the best to use. Some people say that Mexican beer is best, and I knew one fellow who insisted on dark German beer. A few women, on the other hand, prefer a light beer, which they say makes a lighter bread. Personally, I prefer to drink the beer rather than putting it into bread. Suit yourself.

Black Butter Sauce

Here's a sauce that goes nicely with broiled, poached, or sautéed trout. When using the skillet in which trout were pan-fried, purists will insist on having fresh butter for the sauce.

> ¼ cup butter
> ½ tablespoon vinegar
> ½ teaspoon minced parsley leaves

Heat the butter in a skillet until it browns. Remove the skillet from the heat. Mix in the vinegar and parsley. Put back on the heat for 1 minute, stirring with a wooden spoon. Serve hot over fish.

Anchovy Butter

This sauce goes nicely with grilled trout, especially steaks from large trout.

> ¼ cup butter
> 2 or 3 canned anchovy fillets
> juice of ½ lemon

Melt the butter in a skillet. Mash the anchovies with mortar and pestle or in a small bowl with a spoon. Stir the mashed anchovies into the melted butter, then mix in the lemon juice. Serve the butter warm over grilled trout, or use the sauce as a baste during the last minute or two of cooking.

Cold Dill Sauce

Although this sauce calls for sour cream, you can substitute plain yogurt if you prefer. Also, dried dill can be used if you don't have fresh on hand, but reduce the measure by half.

> 1 cup sour cream
> juice of 1 lemon
> ½ teaspoon chopped fresh dill
> ½ teaspoon salt

Mix all the ingredients, then refrigerate. Serve cold over chilled poached trout or salmon.

Cucumber Sauce

Years ago, my wife went on a diet that seemed to call for lots of cucumber and yogurt. That's when I first stirred up this sauce, and we still eat it from time to time. It's best to avoid the very large cucumbers and to use the small ones whole instead of peeling them. That way, the minced green peelings add some color to the sauce.

> ½ cup minced cucumber
> ¼ cup low-fat yogurt
> ¼ teaspoon celery salt
> ¼ teaspoon salt
> ¼ teaspoon white pepper

Mince the cucumber, then drain it well. Then mix all the ingredients and set aside for a few minutes before serving. This sauce goes nicely with poached or broiled trout. It is also ideal for use in a seafood salad with chunks of poached trout.

Dill Sauce with Low-Fat Yogurt

Here's a sauce to serve whenever part of the company to be fed is on a low-fat diet and another part doesn't care for cucumbers. This sauce goes nicely over grilled or broiled trout. If fresh dill isn't readily available, substitute ½ tablespoon of dried.

> 8 ounces plain low-fat yogurt
> 1 tablespoon grated onion
> 1 tablespoon minced fresh dill
> ½ teaspoon white pepper

Mix all the ingredients, then chill for several hours before serving.

Hot Creole Sauce

Here's a Caribbean sauce that goes nicely as a topping for poached or baked fish.

> 1 large tomato, peeled and chopped
> 1 large onion, minced
> 1 fresh chili pepper, seeded and minced
> 3 tablespoons olive oil
> 1 tablespoon vinegar
> salt and freshly ground black pepper

Heat the olive oil in a skillet, and sauté the onion for a few minutes. Add the tomato, chili pepper, salt, and black pepper. Cook for 5 minutes, stirring constantly. Stir in the vinegar and serve.

Note: Add a little more chili pepper if you want a very hot sauce, or reduce the measure to ½ pepper if you want a milder one. Also, a good deal depends on the size and kind of pepper. My last batch of this recipe was made with a little, round pepper that I found in a bag of parrot feed; a Korean lady at the store where I bought it said it was a Korean pepper. I don't know. The parrot wouldn't eat it, and my wife planted the seeds. The resulting pepper pods are the size of a marble, tasty, and hot as hell.

Ham Sauce for Fish

Here's a recipe to use whenever you don't have quite enough fish to feed everybody. It is tasty and quite filling.

> ¼ cup cured ham, minced
> 2 medium tomatoes, peeled and chopped
> 1 medium onion, diced
> ½ green bell pepper, seeded and diced
> ½ red bell pepper, seeded and diced
> 3 cloves garlic, minced
> 2 tablespoons olive oil
> ½ tablespoon brown sugar
> ½ teaspoon salt, or to taste
> ½ teaspoon Spanish (hot) paprika

Heat the oil in a skillet, and sauté the onion, bell peppers, garlic, and ham for 10 minutes, stirring with a wooden spoon. Add the chopped tomato, sugar, salt, and paprika. Simmer for 30 minutes. Serve hot with cooked trout.

Egg Sauce

This basic mild-flavored sauce goes nicely with poached fish, and it can be made with some of the poaching liquid or with Court Bouillon instead of Fish Stock. Egg Sauce is also good with grilled or broiled fish, in which case it should be made with Fish Stock (recipe appears later in this chapter).

> 1 cup Fish Stock
> 3 tablespoons butter
> 3 tablespoons flour
> 2 chicken egg yolks

Start with the eggs at room temperature. Separate the egg yolks, and discard the whites or save them for another recipe. Beat the yolks in a bowl. In a saucepan or small skillet, melt the butter, and stir in the flour with a wooden spoon. Gradually stir in the Fish Stock. Remove the pan from the heat, and gradually pour the contents into the egg yolks, stirring as you go. Pour the mixture back into the skillet, and heat for about 1 minute, but do not boil. Serve the Egg Sauce hot.

Court Bouillon

This is a French recipe for making a liquid in which to poach fish. There are many similar recipes, usually containing onions, carrots, and celery. The liquid is strained and used to poach the fish. Often it is stored in jars for future use. After poaching the fish in the Court Bouillon, the liquid can then be used as stock for making various sauces. The idea is used in many parts of the world to add flavor to fish. The Court Bouillon below, as good as any, is an old New England recipe. The first 3 ingredients are set forth in ⅓ cups. Any mix of these yielding 1 full cup will be satisfactory, but I prefer to go heavy on the celery if I have a choice.

⅓ cup chopped onion
⅓ cup chopped celery
⅓ cup chopped carrots
1 tablespoon chopped fresh parsley
2 bay leaves
6 whole cloves
6 peppercorns
3 tablespoons butter
½ cup red wine vinegar
2 quarts water

Put 2 quarts of water into a stock pot and turn on the heat. In a skillet, heat the butter and sauté the carrots, celery, and onions. Add the skillet contents and the rest of the ingredients to the boiling water. Bring to a new boil, and simmer for 30 minutes. Strain the liquid, and use immediately or store in jars, refrigerated. If you freeze the Court Bouillon, consider using plastic containers instead of jars.

Fish Stock

Never throw out a trout head or the backbone left from filleting the fish. Both can be used to make Fish Stock, which is used in a number of recipes not only for trout, but also for other fish. It can also be used as a soup or as the base for a soup. So make up a batch of stock whenever you clean fish, and freeze it if you don't have an immediate use for it.

> 4 pounds trout heads and bony pieces
> 2 quarts water
> 2 cups dry white wine
> 1 medium onion, chopped
> 1 rib celery with green top, chopped
> 1 carrot, chopped
> ½ cup chopped fresh parsley
> 3 bay leaves
> 10 peppercorns

Put all of the ingredients except the wine into a stock pot. Bring to a boil, and simmer for 1 hour. Strain the liquid, and put it back into the pot. Add the wine, and simmer until the volume is reduced by half. This recipe makes about 4 cups of stock. Use it immediately, refrigerate it for several days, or freeze it for future use. It's most useful to freeze the stock in 1-cup units.

Most cooks throw out the vegetables and fish heads, but I like to nibble on the discards. The heads contain some very tasty meat, especially if you sprinkle on a little salt.

Onion Sauce

I like to serve this sauce over broiled trout fillets. It can also be used to baste the fish toward the end of the broiling or grilling process. Use it sparingly as a marinade. It's best to use a mild-flavored onion.

> ½ cup olive oil
> 1 medium onion, grated
> juice of 1 lemon
> 1 teaspoon prepared mustard
> salt and pepper to taste

Mix together the olive oil, lemon juice, mustard, salt, and pepper. Grate the onion, stir it in, and set aside for ½ hour or longer. If you are in a hurry, first chop the onion, and then zap it in a food processor. Add the other ingredients, and zap it again. Or, instead of creating a mess in the food processor, puree the onion with a high-speed hand-held mixer, then mix in the other ingredients.

Oyster Sauce for Fish

If you have fresh oysters, consider making this tasty sauce to go over fish. It's from an early American cookbook called *The Virginia Housewife*, first published in 1742—back when oysters were available in great plenty. These days, if you have to purchase fresh oysters, you'll probably want to cut the measures in half.

"Scald a pint of oysters, and strain them through a sieve; then wash some more in cold water, and take off their beards; put them in a stew-pan, and pour the liquor over them; then add a large spoonful of anchovy liquor, half a lemon, two blades of mace, and thicken it with butter rolled in flour; put in half a pound of butter, and boil it till it is melted—take out the mace and lemon, and squeeze the lemon juice into the sauce; boil it, and stir it all the time, and put it in a boat."

I don't quite know what anchovy liquor is, but I have used 1 teaspoon of anchovy paste in the recipe with great results.

Shallot Wine Sauce

This recipe requires a double boiler and a little patience. The sauce is worth the effort, however, and it can be served over baked, poached, steamed, or broiled fish. I have adapted the recipe from Milo Miloradovich's *Cooking with Herbs and Spices*.

> 1 cup dry white wine
> ½ cup heavy cream
> 3 tablespoons melted butter
> 2 tablespoons tomato paste
> 1 tablespoon tarragon vinegar
> 3 chicken egg yolks
> 1 tablespoon minced shallots
> 1 teaspoon minced fresh parsley
> ½ teaspoon minced fresh tarragon
> 6 white peppercorns, crushed

In a saucepan, bring the wine, vinegar, shallots, parsley, tarragon, and crushed peppercorns to a rapid boil. Reduce the heat, and simmer for about ½ hour, or until the liquid is reduced by half. Remove from heat and let cool. Boil a little water in the bottom unit of a double boiler. Strain the liquid from the saucepan into the top section of the double boiler. One at a time, beat each egg yolk and stir it into the liquid, along with 1 tablespoon of the butter for each egg yolk. Finally, stir in the tomato paste and cream. Stir well, heating through, and serve hot.

Tomato Sauce

This sauce goes well with trout cooked in any style. I am especially fond of it spooned sparingly over broiled trout. Be sure to try it with broiled lake trout fillets. For best results, use home-grown tomatoes. Purists will insist on peeling and seeding the tomatoes, but I confess that I leave the seeds in. To peel the tomatoes easily, stick them with a fork and immerse them into boiling water for about 10 seconds. The skins will then slip off.

3 large tomatoes, peeled and chopped
1 large onion, finely chopped
2 cloves garlic, minced
¼ cup butter
1 teaspoon fresh thyme, minced
salt and pepper

Melt the butter in a skillet, then sauté the onion and garlic for 5 minutes. Add the chopped tomato, thyme, salt, and pepper. Increase the heat until the contents bubble, reduce the heat, and simmer uncovered for 30 minutes.

Note: If you don't have fresh thyme on hand, use ½ teaspoon dried thyme. Also add a little rosemary if you have it.

Horseradish Sauce

This sauce is especially good with poached fish, and it makes use of part of the poaching liquid. (You can also use Fish Stock; the recipe appears earlier in this chapter.) The recipe calls for grated fresh horseradish roots. If you plan to make a large batch of this sauce, increase the measures and zap the horseradish in a food processor instead of grating it.

1 cup grated fresh horseradish
2 cups Fish Stock or poaching liquid
1 cup butter
1 cup whipping cream
1 cup soft bread crumbs
3 hard-boiled chicken egg yolks
1 tablespoon Creole or Dijon mustard
salt
Tabasco sauce

Bring the Fish Stock or poaching liquid to a boil in a saucepan, add the horseradish, and simmer for 20 minutes. Add the butter, cream, and bread crumbs. Season with salt and a little Tabasco sauce. Bring almost to a boil, then turn off the heat. Mash the egg yolks and prepared mustard, then stir the mixture into the sauce. Serve over poached or steamed fish.

Easy Horseradish Sauce

If you don't want to make a real sauce, you san simply add grated horseradish to the pan drippings after sautéing trout in butter. Stir in a little cream, sour cream, or plain yogurt, if available, and season with salt and white pepper. Add lemon juice if desired. Grated horseradish also can be added to mayonnaise or other sauces. It will add some punch to store-bought tartar sauce.

Onion Butter

Most Americans don't realize how much we depend on onions in our fish and meat recipes. I read somewhere about someone starting each recipe with, "Take an onion . . ." I am especially fond of cooking with sautéed onions not only because I like the flavor, but also because I like to smell them cooking. Even people who don't like to eat onions should consider using more of them in their cookery. In any case, here's a hot butter sauce that I like to use over fish, and I have been guilty of using the sauce as a medium for pan-frying or sautéing a trout or two.

> ½ cup butter
> juice of ½ lemon
> ½ cup minced green onions with half of tops
> salt and pepper to taste

Heat the butter in a skillet or saucepan. Sauté the minced green onions for 5 minutes on low heat. Stir in the lemon juice, salt, and pepper. Serve warm over poached or broiled trout.

Note: Try the above recipe with wild onions and about half of their green tops. There are many varieties of wild onions and garlics, and most of them have a wonderful flavor, but they are on the strong side. Add more butter if you've got too much of a good thing.

Tartar Sauce

There must be a thousand recipes for this famous sauce. It can be used with almost any seafood, and it is popular as a dip for deep-fried fish. It can be purchased at the supermarket, but it's really easy to make your own if you've got good mayonnaise. This recipe calls for minced red bell pepper. This ingredient is used here mostly for color and really isn't a conventional ingredient for this sauce. Omit it if you wish.

> 1 cup mayonnaise
> 2 tablespoons minced onion
> 2 tablespoons minced red bell pepper (optional)
> 2 tablespoons minced dill pickle
> 2 tablespoons minced fresh parsley
> 1 tablespoon bottled capers

Mix all the ingredients in a bowl. Refrigerate until time to eat. Serve in a sauce bowl, or put portions in individual serving cups.

Variation: Omit the red bell pepper, and use 1 tablespoon chopped stuffed olives.

Dill Butter

Here's a butter that goes nicely with baked or broiled fish. It can be kept refrigerated until needed.

> ¼ pound butter
> 2 tablespoons ground dill seeds
> 1 tablespoon minced fresh parsley
> juice of 1 lemon
> ½ teaspoon salt
> ¼ teaspoon white pepper
> ⅛ teaspoon cayenne

Bring the butter to room temperature, then mash it with a spoon, adding the salt, white pepper, cayenne, dill seeds, and

133

parsley. Mix in the lemon juice, then set aside for 1 to 2 hours for the flavors to mingle. Then refrigerate until needed. Slice and place the butter on individual servings of baked or broiled fish. Or melt the butter and baste the fish during the last minute or two of cooking.

APPENDIX A

Ten Steps to Better Trout

You can almost always catch a better fish than you can buy. On the other hand, farmed rainbow and even brown trout, as well as salmon, are becoming more widely available in our markets. Some of these are sold whole; others are butterflied. Some are fresh, some frozen. So most Americans can enjoy trout these days. My stand is that a farmed trout may not be as good as a wild trout, but it's better than no trout at all, if it has been handled properly during the marketing stage.

Nevertheless, catching your own is still the best way to go. For one thing, you can get the whole trout, which can be important for making stock and for obtaining the roe, liver, and other good parts—gourmet eating that goes to waste with most market fish. Many pay-to-fish ponds are stocked with trout, and more and more urban fishing programs feature trout fishing, even in areas where trout don't reproduce in the local waters.

In any case, here are some pointers to keep in mind for better eating.

1. The fresher the trout, the better. Freshly caught trout from a good stream are about as good as fish get, in my opinion. The small fish—8- or 9-inchers—are better than larger ones for some methods of cooking. Stocked hatchery trout may not be quite as good as truly wild trout, but they are nevertheless delectable. Even fish freshly caught from pay-to-fish pools are very good. The main advantage of catching your own is that you know they are fresh, you know the water they came from, and you have full control over how they are handled from the water to the table. It's usually best to cook the fish as soon as they are taken from the water, in my opinion.

In some cases, it may be practical to keep the fish alive until you are ready to cook them. Usually, however, it is better to follow step 2 rather than trying to keep the fish alive on a stringer or in a live well of a boat. If you do use a stringer, use one with large snaps, and hook the fish through the lips instead of stringing them up through the gill and out the mouth. If you wade, you can sometimes keep your fish alive in a large creek simply by making sure they stay partly submerged in the water.

If trout are put on ice shortly after being caught, they can be kept for several days. It is also quite possible to buy very fresh fish in markets, but this is always a gamble. The best bet is to gain the confidence of a competent dealer. Fresh fish have firm flesh and bright eyes. Books and magazine articles tell us not to buy fish that smell fishy. Also, they say, the eyes should be clear and the gills red. In most markets around the country, the fish are displayed on ice and have been beheaded, so you won't be able to see the eyes or the gills. Also, I seldom feel free to poke fish with my fingers, and I hesitate to ask the dealer to take the fish out of the case so that I can smell it. If you can't catch your trout, the best bet is to find a good fish market, gain the confidence of a clerk, and put your faith in him or her. Usually, the fresh trout on sale in a market will be farmed rainbows. Sometimes these will be sold live from tanks. I recommend that you take them home live and dress them youself.

Unless you can buy live trout, I suggest you get fish that have been frozen while very fresh and shipped to market in frozen form. Some writers have claimed that frozen trout are terrible and tasteless, but I don't see it that way.

But the best bet is still to catch your own fish. That way you'll know what you've got. A wild fish is usually better than a farmed fish, be it trout, salmon, or catfish.

2. Keep the fish cool. If you can't cook the fish right away, keep it cool. This is best accomplished with an ice chest, but a good creel with a little wet moss in it can help keep trout cool on a stream. When using a creel, however, it's best to draw the fish.

If I have plenty of ice, I seldom draw or dress trout right away. It's best to keep the water drained from the bottom of the ice chest.

3. Do not skin or scale until necessary. Most of the trouts and salmons have very small scales and are usually not scaled at all before cooking. In some cases, it's best to cook the fish with the skin (and scales) intact, and then remove the skin after cooking. It's always best to leave the skin on as long as possible simply because it holds in the juices. Larger trout to be used in soups, stews, or flaked fish dishes usually should be skinned before cooking. Also, if an off taste is caused by excessive algae in the water (as discussed in appendix B), skinning may help the flavor of the trout.

4. Dress the fish properly. Always dress a trout according to the way you are going to cook it. I like small trout cooked whole—head, tails, skin, scales, and fins. Others prefer them beheaded, and some people even cut off the fins with scissors.

If fillets are called for in a recipe, I generally recommend boneless fillets, although for my own use I usually leave the rib bones intact. To fillet a fish with the rib bones, start filleting at the tail with a sharp knife and work toward the head, cutting through the rib bones when you get to them. If you like, you can cut out the bones after filleting. If you want boneless fillets, it's really best to start from the top, working the point of a small, short-bladed knife (not a fillet knife) along the backbone to the rib cage, then along the rib cage to the belly; at the end of the rib cage, work the knife all the way through the surface of the skin at the bottom of the fish and back toward the tail.

I've seen several books with recipes calling for whole boned trout. Frankly, I never attempt to bone a trout, and I don't expect my readers to, either. Some writers haul off and describe it, all right—telling you how to do the wrong thing, it seems to me. Consider the following excerpt from *How to Cook His Goose* by Karen Green and Betty Black. (I have seen almost the same description elsewhere.)

Lay the fish on a flat surface, open the body cavity (which has previously been gutted), and insert a sharp knife under the backbone at the head. Carefully cut between the ribs and the flesh. Do not cut through the back of the fish and break the skin. Release the bones from the back of the fish. Repeat the operation on the other side of the trout. You should then be able to remove the whole bone structure in one piece.

The illustration to the above text shows a knife going in from the bottom and under the bottom of the rib cage. The left hand is magically pulling the flesh away from the top of the rib cage! If you really want to bone a fish, start the process before gutting it. Leave the head and tail on the fish, and start the boning process on the top near the head with the fish on its side. Run your knife blade as closely as possible to the backbone so that you won't lose much meat. Work carefully along the rib cage, where the meat will be very thin. After cutting around the rib cage, work toward the tail, working all the way to the skin on the bottom. Turn the fish over and do the other side. Sever the spinal column at the head and again at the tail. Then lift out the backbone, ribs, and innards. Notice that the belly is left intact, so that the fish will hold together. It can then be stuffed and baked, or cooked in one way or another.

Nevertheless, I simply don't recommend boning a whole trout. It's easier to do this after the fish has been cooked, or to use boneless fillets. Also, be warned that boning a fish will leave some of the fins intact—and the fins of some spiny-rayed fish, such as largemouth and smallmouth bass, have some mean bones going down into the flesh.

5. Freeze quickly and properly. If you are going to freeze your trout, do so as soon as you can. Generally, fish are better if they are frozen in a solid block of ice, although this is not always practical, and it takes a lot of freezer space. If at all possible, also freeze fillets in this manner. A ½-gallon milk carton is usually ideal for this purpose.

Large fish can frozen whole, with skin and scales. Sometimes they are dipped in water and quickly frozen to form a glaze on the surface. They can also be put into plastic tubes and frozen, which I highly recommend. If you don't have a plastic tube (available from suppliers who deal in packaging materials), wrap the fish as best you can with plastic film, then wrap it again in aluminum foil. In any case, it's best to leave the scales and skin on a fish when freezing it whole, as they help protect the flesh. Believe it or not, I sometimes freeze large fish whole, without even drawing them. Why? A whole fish is more versatile. I can use it whole, fillet it, or cut it into steaks, depending on how I decide to cook it.

It's best to thaw fish very slowly. Most experts recommend that you put them into a refrigerator overnight. This is fine if you know a day ahead that you will need the fish. Most people, however, including this writer, often wind up thawing the fish at room temperature—and sometimes with the help of running water. Just remember that slower is better, then do what you have to do to feed everybody on time.

6. Cook by an appropriate method. As pointed out earlier, some fatty fish do not fry successfully. Some wild species are in this category, except for small specimens. Water conditions, especially temperature, also have a bearing on how fatty a fish is. Fatty fish are usually at their best when smoked or grilled, but generalizations are not entirely accurate because some fatty fish are milder in flavor. See appendix B for some rules of thumb for the various trouts and other salmonoids.

Of course, the kind of meal you are planning should have a bearing on your choice of recipes. Having a formal meal doesn't necessarily mean, however, that you have to spend two days making French sauces. Trout don't need complicated sauces in order to be good; in my opinion, they are usually better when cooked simply.

7. Be careful about cooking whole fish. Although I always like trout with the heads on (unless they are too large to go into the pan), some people have other feelings on this matter. If in doubt, always remove the heads either before or after cooking, but before showing the fish to your guests.

8. Do not overcook. From a culinary standpoint, one of the worst things you can do to a fish is to overcook it. When fried, grilled, or broiled, overcooked fish becomes dry, chewy, and tasteless. Even boiling fish too long is not good, and it's always better to poach a fish in simmering water rather than at a rolling boil.

As trout has a higher fat content than cod or bass, it's more fool-proof, but, even so, it is better when properly cooked.

9. Pay careful attention to detail. Trout is at its best in a simple recipe with only a few ingredients. It is therefore essential that the ingredients are of top quality and are properly used. Fresh parsley, for instance, is available in most supermarkets and from home gardens and is always better for flavor and for garnish than the dried herb. Also, some simple recipes and cooking techniques have to be followed exactly in order to work properly; for example, the Blue Trout recipe won't work if the skin of the fish is scrubbed.

10. Choose your guests carefully. If you've got to feed somebody who turns up his or her nose at the very mention of the word *fish,* or who talks about fish smelling up the house, serve the person hamburger, thereby saving your good brook trout for yourself.

Guide to the Trouts and Their Cousins

In some cases, it's hard to tell what's a trout and what's a char or salmon or grayling, and experts argue among themselves over the various classifications. Even if I could straighten all this out, the result would be a quagmire. Instead, I have decided to include the more popular kinds of all these fish. It would be difficult to exclude some of those that are not trout from a technical viewpoint. The popular brook trout, for example, is a really a char—but to leave the brook trout out of this book would be a culinary sin.

Remember that some trout and other salmonoids are not always at their best. As a rule, those that make long runs upstream to spawn are better for eating purposes at the beginning of the run than at the end. Also, the fat content of some of the salmonoids depends on the water temperature and other factors. Of course, the size of the fish is also a consideration. As a rule, the smaller fish are better for eating, especially for frying, but this rule does not always hold. I have also read that too much algae in the water can cause trout to have an off flavor. I have never experienced the problem, and I consider it to be temporary.

Arctic Char. This circumpolar char lives in the Far North, including Siberia. The color of the flesh varies from yellowish to fire red, depending on habitat. The fish is best when smoked, but it can be grilled or broiled with excellent results. Do not fry it, however. In some barren lands, such as Iceland, the fish is smoked over a fire made with dried sheep dung.

American Grayling. This beautiful cold-water troutlike fish

141

is found mostly in Canada, Alaska, and Siberia. It has firm white flesh that can be cooked satisfactorily by any means. The European grayling is also excellent table fare. The flesh of the American grayling smells rather like thyme, hence the scientific name *Thymallus thymallus*.

Atlantic Salmon. This great sport fish is on the oily side, but it makes excellent eating when it is smoked, grilled, broiled, poached, or canned. The small ones can be fried. The fish is found in the northern part of the Atlantic, from Cape Cod to Russia. In Maine and some parts of Canada, the fish has become landlocked. (These landlocked fish are sometimes called *sebago salmon.*) Small salmon returning from salt water are sometimes called *grilse.*

Brook Trout. A char, this fish makes excellent table fare. The small ones are ideal for pan frying or sautéing. Large ones can be baked, broiled, grilled, smoked, or poached. It is usually best to leave the skin on the fish, and some people say that the skin should not be washed too thoroughly since the slimy coating adds to the flavor and color.

Brown Trout. Native to Europe and Siberia, the brown trout has been stocked successfully in North America, South America, Africa, New Zealand, and perhaps other places. The brown is highly regarded both as a game fish and as table fare, and it is now farmed commercially. There are a number of subspecies, such as the gillaroo of Ireland, a fish that has red flesh, and a Turkish variation, *Allah balik,* or "God's fish." The Kura strain of the Caspian Sea spawns only once during its lifetime and may weigh as much as 112 pounds.

Char. This large group of salmonoids includes the Dolly Varden, lake trout, and brook trout, as well as the arctic char. These are discussed separately.

Chum Salmon. This salmon has a very high oil content and is usually used only for grilling or smoking. It is a Pacific salmon, ranging from California to Japan. It has also been stocked by the Russians in Barents Sea and has become established in the streams all the way to Norway.

Coho Salmon. This excellent fish, with medium oil content, can be cooked by any method and is especially good for smoking. For frying, the fish should be filleted and cut into fingers. The coho is also called *silver salmon* and *hooknose*. It is popular in the Pacific Northwest and has been successfully introduced into the Great Lakes.

Cutthroat Trout. A fish of medium oil content and mild flavor, the cutthroat can be cooked by any method. The flesh varies from white to red.

Dolly Varden. This char has a pink or reddish, somewhat oily flesh that is excellent when grilled, broiled, or smoked. The fish ranges from California, across the Northern Pacific, on down to Korea. The name comes from a fictional character who wore a pink spotted dress in a novel by Charles Dickens.

Golden Trout. This beautiful fish from the headwaters of the Kern River of California has been stocked successfully in several other states. Its firm white flesh is a little oily and doesn't keep too well; but when fresh it is very good and can be cooked by any method. It is best when pan-fried along a stream or when smoked.

Green Trout. An old regional name for largemouth and other black bass.

Hybrid Trout. Fishery biologists have developed several hybrid trouts for one reason or another. A hybrid brook trout and lake trout is called a *splake*. The *sp* part of the name comes from "speckled trout," as brook trout are called in Canada. The *trousal* is a cross between a brown trout and an Atlantic salmon. Several other hybrids have been developed, but none of these experiments improve on the fish as table fare.

Inconnu. Also called *sheefish* and *connie*, these members of the Salmonidae family are prized as gamefish in parts of Alaska. They are edible, but are not highly prized as table fare.

Kokanee. A landlocked sockeye, this oily fish deteriorates quickly and should be iced as soon as it is caught. It is best when smoked and should not be fried or baked. The kokanee is sometimes called *red salmon* or *redfish*.

Lake Trout. Called *togue* in the Northeast, *mackinaw* in the West, and *gray trout* in parts of Canada, this large char inhabits deep cold-water lakes of the northern United States and Canada, as well as some of the large streams connected to such lakes. Sport fishermen often take lake trout by trolling in suitable waters. It is also available commercially in some areas, especially in Canada. The meat—on the oily side—should be refrigerated as soon as possible after the fish is caught and dressed. The lake trout is good for broiling, grilling, and smoking. It can also be poached or steamed, but it isn't ideal for frying. The fish grows to 100 pounds or better. Surprisingly, the larger fish are often better than the small ones.

Pacific Salmon. The six species of Pacific salmon include the chinook, the coho, the sockeye, the pink, the chum, and the cherry. This last species is available only in Asia.

Pink Salmon. This fish is excellent eating. Although it is oily, it can be cooked by any method. It is especially good when smoked.

Rainbow Trout. This popular fish, native to North America, has been stocked in various parts of the world and is now farmed commercially. According to *McClane's New Standard Fishing Encyclopedia and International Angling Guide,* the rainbow's original range was from the mountains of northern Mexico up to the Aleutian Islands, and possibly into eastern Russia (where it is known as the *Kamchatka trout*). When migrating, the rainbow is known as the *steelhead.* Its cream-colored flesh is slightly to moderately oily, but it has a mild flavor and can be cooked by any method, including frying. The wild rainbows are better than the hatchery put-and-take trout—and the latter are better that those that are farmed and fattened for the market.

Salmon. Most of the salmons are best when smoked, poached, grilled, or broiled. Do not fry, except perhaps for smaller specimens. Several salmon species are covered in this section.

Sea Trout. An anadromous form of the brown trout. Also, the term is often applied to the speckled sea trout (or "spec"), a popular sport and food fish of the Gulf of Mexico; most New Orleans "trout" recipes are for this fish, which isn't a real trout.

The silver sea trout, the sand sea trout (or white sea trout), and the spotted sea trout are members of the drum family.

Sockeye Salmon. Although it has a high oil content, this mild fish can be prepared by any method, including frying. It is ideal for smoking.

A number of other trout species exist, but these are of minor importance except to some local areas. The Sunapee, for example, may be a distinct species from Sunapee Lake in New Hampshire. The Gila trout is native to the Gila River in New Mexico and Arizona. The blueback trout is present today in only a few lakes in Maine.

There are other fish known as *trout* in some areas. In the American South, the black bass has been called *trout* or *green trout* for a long time, although this has changed considerably during the past fifty years, and the cypress trout is actually a bowfin.

APPENDIX C

Metric Conversion Tables

U.S. Standard measurements for cooking use ounces, pounds, pints, quarts, gallons, teaspoons, tablespoons, cups, and fractions thereof. The following tables enable those who use the metric system to easily convert the U.S. Standard measurements to metric.

Weights

U.S. Standard	Metric	U.S. Standard	Metric
.25 ounce	7.09 grams	11 ounces	312 grams
.50	14.17	12	340
.75	21.26	13	369
1	28.35	14	397
2	57	15	425
3	85	1 pound	454
4	113	2	907
5	142	2.2	1 kilogram
6	170	4.4	2
7	198	6.6	3
8	227	8.8	4
9	255	11.0	5
10	283		

Liquids

U.S. Standard	Metric	U.S. Standard	Metric
1/8 teaspoon	.61 milliliter	3/8 cup	90 milliliters
1/4	1.23	1/2	120
1/2	2.50	2/3	160
3/4	3.68	3/4	180
1	4.90	7/8	210
2	10	1	240
1 tablespoon	15	2	480
2	30	3	720
1/4 cup	60	4	960
1/3	80	5	1200

To convert	multiply	by
Ounces to milliliters	the ounces	30
Teaspoons to milliliters	the teaspoons	5
Tablespoons to milliliters	the tablespoons	15
Cups to liters	the cups	.24
Pints to liters	the pints	.47
Quarts to liters	the quarts	.95
Gallons to liters	the gallons	3.8
Ounces to grams	the ounces	28.35
Pounds to kilograms	the pounds	.45
Inches to centimeters	the inches	2.54

To convert Fahrenheit to Celsius: Subtract 32, multiply by 5, divide by 9.

Index